Welcome Home
AMERICAN CLASSICS

Welcome Home
AMERICAN CLASSICS

FAVORITE RECIPES FROM ACROSS THE COUNTRY

Photos by Bonnie Matthews

New York, New York

Photos by Bonnie Matthews

Good Books books may be purchased in bulk at special discounts for sales promotion, corporate gifts, fund-raising, or educational purposes. Special editions can also be created to specifications. For details, contact the Special Sales Department, Good Books, 307 West 36th Street, 11th Floor, New York, NY 10018 or info@skyhorsepublishing.com.

Good Books is an imprint of Skyhorse Publishing, Inc.®, a Delaware corporation.

Visit our website at www.goodbooks.com.

10 9 8 7 6 5 4 3 2 1

Library of Congress Cataloging-in-Publication Data is available on file.

Cover design by Kai Texel
Cover photo by Bonnie Matthews

Print ISBN: 978-1-964219-07-3
Ebook ISBN: 978-1-964219-24-0

Printed in China

Table of Contents

About Welcome Home American Classics

Welcome! In these pages, you will find 127 of the best all-American inspired recipes from home cooks like you! Whether you're from the Northeast, Southeast, Midwest, Southwest, or the West, hopefully you'll find a little piece of home here. With recipes like Finger-Lickin' Spareribs, Smoky Brisket, Oven-Fried Catfish, Jiffy Jambalaya, Beef and Pepperoncini Hoagies, Manhattan Clam Chowder, Southern Pecan Pie, Fresh Peach Pie, and so much more, we hope you'll be inspired to visit someplace new . . . even if it's just in the comfort of your own kitchen!

As you begin journeying through this book, I always suggest reading it from cover to cover. I can't tell you the good recipes I've passed on in the past by not following this advice. Don't become overwhelmed. Bookmark or dog-ear the pages of the recipes that you think your family would enjoy the most, can be made with ingredients you have around the house, or fit with their dietary needs. Then, when you've looked at everything, go back to those marked pages and narrow it down. Make yourself a grocery list and grab what you don't already have. Voilà! You're ready to get cooking! Your kitchen is about to experience deliciousness from all over the United States. So, get cookin'!

Breakfasts

Blueberry Pancakes

Becky Frey, Lebanon, PA

Makes 15 medium-sized pancakes, or 4–5 servings

Prep. Time: 10–15 minutes *Cooking Time: 10 minutes*

- 2 eggs
- 1 cup buttermilk
- ¼ cup oil
- 1 tsp. almond extract
- 2 cups whole wheat (or white) flour
- 2 Tbsp. brown sugar
- 2 tsp. baking powder
- 1 tsp. baking soda
- 1 cup fresh blueberries

1. In large mixing bowl beat eggs until fluffy.
2. Stir buttermilk, oil, and almond extract into eggs.
3. In a separate bowl, combine flour, brown sugar, baking powder, and baking soda. Add to wet ingredients. Beat together with whisk just until smooth.
4. Heat skillet or griddle until a few drops of water sizzle when sprinkled on top.
5. Pour ¼–⅓ cup of batter onto hot surface for each pancake. Drop in a few blueberries to each pancake.
6. Fry pancakes until bubbly on top. Flip and continue cooking until browned. Turn the heat lower if necessary if they start to scorch or burn.

Tip:

You can use fresh or frozen berries. If frozen, thaw them and drain them well before adding.

Serving suggestion:

Top finished pancakes with vanilla yogurt and fruit sauce and serve for breakfast, brunch, a light lunch, or supper, or as a dessert.

Sourdough Pancakes

Melissa Paskvan, Novi, MI

Makes about 10 small pancakes

Prep. Time: 25 minutes ❧ *Cooking Time: approximately 9 minutes*

1½ cups milk (or nondairy milk)
2 Tbsp. vanilla extract
1 egg
2 Tbsp. sourdough starter
1 Tbsp. oil of your choice
1 cup all-purpose flour
1 Tbsp. baking powder
1 tsp. salt
1–2 Tbsp. of cane sugar or maple sugar

1. Mix wet ingredients in a small bowl.
2. Sift the dry ingredients together in a medium-sized mixing bowl.
3. Add the liquids to the dry ingredients and mix just enough. Do not overmix.
4. Let the mixture sit for 15 mins.
5. Preheat a large nonstick skillet to medium-low heat.
6. Pour in ¼–⅓ cup of batter for each pancake into the pan. Cook for 1–2 minutes, then when the edges begin to bubble, flip them over and cook for approximately one more minute.

Variation:

These can be made vegan by replacing the egg with flax egg.

Peach Cobbler Coffee Cake

Jean Butzer, Batavia, NY

Makes 15–20 servings

Prep. Time: 20 minutes · *Baking Time: 60–70 minutes* · *Cooling Time: 30 minutes*

- 21-oz. can peach pie filling
- 16-oz. can sliced peaches, drained well
- 1 cup brown sugar
- 4 cups flour, *divided*
- ½ cup dry quick oats
- 3 sticks (1½ cups) butter, softened, *divided*
- 1 cup sugar
- 1¼ cups sour cream
- 2 eggs, slightly beaten
- 1 Tbsp. vanilla extract
- 1 tsp. baking powder
- 1 tsp. baking soda
- ½ tsp. salt
- 1 cup confectioners' sugar
- 1–2 Tbsp. milk

1. In a medium-sized mixing bowl, stir together pie filling and sliced peaches. Set aside.

2. In another mixing bowl, mix the brown sugar, 1 cup flour, and oats. Cut in 1 stick (½ cup) butter with a pastry cutter until mixture resembles coarse crumbs. Set aside to use as topping.

3. In a large electric mixer bowl, beat together 2 sticks (1 cup) butter and sugar until creamy. Add sour cream, eggs, and vanilla. Beat until well mixed.

4. Reduce speed to low and gradually add 3 cups flour, baking powder, baking soda, and salt. Beat until well mixed.

5. Spread half the batter into a greased 9 × 13-inch deep baking pan. Spoon peach filling evenly over batter. Drop spoonfuls of remaining batter over filling. (Do not spread.)

6. Sprinkle with topping mixture from step 2. Bake at 350°F for 60–70 minutes, or until toothpick comes out clean.

7. Cool 30 minutes. Meanwhile, stir together confectioners' sugar and enough milk to make glaze. Drizzle over cooled coffee cake.

Variation:

You may use any fruit (pie filling and canned fruit) of your choice. Just be sure the sliced fruit is well drained.

Tip:

Use a deep pan (at least 2 1/4 inches) since this recipe fills it right to the top.

Biscuits and Gravy the Instant Pot Way

Hope Comerford, Clinton Township, MI

Makes 4 servings

Prep. Time: 5 minutes ❧ *Cooking Time: 16–20 minutes*

Gravy:

1 Tbsp. butter

8 oz. bulk breakfast sausage

3 Tbsp. flour

½ tsp. garlic powder

¼ tsp. sea salt

¼ tsp. black pepper

1½ cups milk

Biscuits:

¾ cup baking mix

⅓ cup milk

¼ tsp. black pepper

¼ tsp. sea salt

1. Set the Instant Pot to the Sauté setting and place the butter in the inner pot to melt.
2. Add in the breakfast sausage and sauté until browned, about 8 minutes.
3. Stir in the flour, garlic powder, sea salt, and pepper.
4. Whisk in the milk, and bring to a simmer, stirring occasionally.
5. Press Cancel on the Instant Pot.
6. In a bowl, mix the biscuit ingredients.
7. Place dollops of the biscuit mixture over the gravy.
8. Secure the lid and set the vent to sealing.
9. Manually set the cook time for 4 minutes.
10. When cook time is up, let the pressure release naturally for 5 minutes, then manually release the remaining pressure.
11. Serve and enjoy!

Country Brunch

Esther J. Mast, Lancaster, PA
Barbara Yoder, Christiana, PA
Ruth Ann Gingrich, New Holland, PA
Lafaye Musser, Denver, PA

Makes 12–15 servings

Prep. Time: 30 minutes ❧ *Chilling Time: 8 hours, or overnight*
Baking Time: 45–60 minutes ❧ *Standing Time: 10–15 minutes*

- 16 slices firm white bread
- 1⅔–2 lb. (2½ cups) cubed ham or browned sausage, drained
- 1 lb. (3 cups) shredded cheddar cheese
- 1 lb. (3 cups) shredded mozzarella cheese
- 8 eggs, beaten
- 3½ cups milk
- ½ tsp. dry mustard
- ¼ tsp. onion powder
- ½ tsp. seasoning salt
- 1 Tbsp. parsley

Topping:

- 3 cups uncrushed cornflakes
- 1 stick (8 Tbsp.) butter, melted

1. Trim crusts from bread and cut slices in half.
2. Grease a 10 × 15-inch baking dish.
3. Layer ingredients in this order: cover bottom of pan with half the bread, top with half the ham, then half the cheddar cheese, and then half the mozzarella cheese.
4. Repeat layers once more.
5. In large mixing bowl, combine eggs, milk, dry mustard, onion powder, seasoning salt, and parsley. Mix well and pour over layers.
6. Cover and refrigerate for 8 hours, or overnight.
7. Remove from refrigerator 30 minutes before baking.
8. Combine cornflakes and butter and sprinkle over casserole.
9. Cover loosely with foil to prevent over-browning. Bake at 375°F for 45 minutes or until cooked through.
10. Remove from oven and let stand 10–15 minutes before cutting into squares.

Gold Rush Brunch

Trish Dick, Ladysmith, WI

Makes 12 servings

Prep. Time: 2 hours ⁂ *Baking Time: 40–45 minutes* ⁂ *Standing Time: 10 minutes*

4 large potatoes, peeled or unpeeled
½ stick (4 Tbsp.) butter, *divided*
2 Tbsp. chopped onion
2 Tbsp. parsley
1 lb. sausage, ham, or bacon
8 eggs, beaten
1 lb. shredded cheddar cheese, *divided*

White sauce:

½ stick (4 Tbsp.) butter
¼ tsp. salt
1¾ cups milk
¼ cup cornstarch
1 cup sour cream, *optional*

1. Boil potatoes until just soft. Cool to room temperature. Refrigerate until chilled through.
2. When potatoes are cold, grate.
3. Melt 2 Tbsp. butter in large skillet. Stir potatoes and onion into skillet. Cook until lightly browned. Toss in parsley.
4. Spread in well-greased 9 × 13-inch baking pan.
5. Brown sausage, ham, or bacon in same skillet. Drain off drippings.
6. Crumble over potato layer in baking pan.
7. Melt 2 Tbsp. butter in skillet. Pour eggs into skillet. Cook, stirring up from the bottom until eggs are scrambled and just set.
8. Layer eggs over meat.
9. Sprinkle with half of shredded cheese.
10. Make white sauce by melting 4 Tbsp. butter in saucepan.
11. Stir in salt, milk, and cornstarch. Stir continually with a wooden spoon until bubbly and thickened.
12. Remove from heat. Stir in sour cream if you wish.
13. Pour white sauce over egg layer in pan.
14. Sprinkle with remaining shredded cheese.
15. Bake at 350°F for 40 minutes. Insert knife blade in center. If it comes out clean, the dish is finished. If it doesn't, continue baking another 5 minutes. Test again with knife blade. Continue cooking—and testing—as needed.
16. Allow to stand 10 minutes before cutting and serving.

Southwestern Egg Casserole

Eileen Eash, Lafayette, CO

Makes 12 servings

Prep. Time: 20–30 minutes · *Baking Time: 35–45 minutes* · *Standing Time: 5–10 minutes*

- 10 eggs
- ½ cup flour
- 1 tsp. baking powder
- ⅛ tsp. salt
- ⅛ tsp. pepper
- 4 cups shredded Monterey Jack, or cheddar, cheese
- 2 cups cottage cheese
- 1 stick (½ cup) butter, melted
- 2 (4-oz.) cans chopped green chilies

1. Beat eggs in a large mixing bowl.
2. In a smaller bowl, combine flour, baking powder, salt, and pepper.
3. Stir into eggs. Batter will be lumpy.
4. Add cheeses, butter, and chilies to batter.
5. Pour into greased 9 × 13-inch baking dish.
6. Bake at 350°F for 35–45 minutes, or until knife inserted near center comes out clean.
7. Let stand 5–10 minutes before cutting.

California Egg Bake

Leona M. Slabaugh, Apple Creek, OH

Makes 2 servings

Prep. Time: 10–15 minutes *Baking Time: 25–30 minutes*

- 3 eggs
- ¼ cup sour cream
- ¼ tsp. salt
- 1 medium tomato, chopped
- 1 green onion, sliced
- ¼ cup shredded cheese

1. In a small bowl, beat eggs, sour cream, and salt.
2. Stir in tomato, onion, and cheese.
3. Pour into greased 2-cup baking dish.
4. Bake at 350°F for 25–30 minutes, or until a knife inserted in center comes out clean.

Country Breakfast Pizza

Zoë Rohrer, Lancaster, PA

Makes 8–10 servings

Prep. Time: 25–30 minutes *Baking Time: 27 minutes*

- 2 Tbsp. butter
- 1 cup whole wheat pastry flour
- ⅔ cup + 2 Tbsp., all-purpose flour
- 1 Tbsp. flax meal, *optional*
- 2 tsp. baking powder
- ½ tsp. salt
- ¼ cup real maple syrup
- Scant ½ cup milk
- ½ green pepper, diced
- ⅔ lb. bulk pork sausage
- 9 large eggs
- 1⅓ cups grated cheddar cheese, *divided*
- Maple syrup, or ketchup, for serving

1. Place butter in a 9 × 13-inch baking dish. Place dish in oven set at 425°F. Keep an eye on butter, and when it's melted (about 5 minutes), take dish out of oven.
2. Meanwhile, in a good-sized bowl, mix the flours, flax if you wish, baking powder, and salt.
3. Add maple syrup and milk. Stir to combine.
4. Knead a few minutes in bowl, or on countertop, to make a ball.
5. Press dough into buttered baking dish.
6. Bake 12 minutes at 425°F. Remove from the oven.
7. While crust is baking, brown sausage and peppers in skillet until pink is gone from meat and peppers are just tender. Stir frequently to break up meat. Place cooked meat and peppers on platter (reserve drippings in skillet) and keep warm.
8. Beat eggs in mixing bowl. Pour into drippings in skillet. Stir frequently.
9. Add ⅔ cup cheese while eggs are cooking.
10. When crust is done, top with sausage, then eggs, and then remaining cheese.
11. Bake 10 more minutes or until cheese is melted.
12. Serve immediately with maple syrup or ketchup.

Eggs California

Vonda Ebersole, Mt. Pleasant Mills, PA
Judy Gonzales, Fishers, IN
Esther Gingerich, Parnell, IA

Makes 10 servings

Prep. Time: 20 minutes ❧ *Baking Time: 40–45 minutes*

- 10 eggs
- 2 cups cottage cheese
- ½ cup flour
- 1 tsp. baking powder
- ½ tsp. salt
- ½ cup melted butter
- 1 lb. shredded cheddar, Swiss, or Monterey Jack cheese
- 1 or 2 (4-oz.) cans chopped green chilies, depending upon your taste preference

1. In a mixing bowl, beat together eggs, cottage cheese, flour, baking powder, salt, and butter.
2. Stir in cheese and green chilies.
3. Pour into a greased 9 × 13-inch baking dish.
4. Bake at 350°F for 40 to 45 minutes, or until set.

Serving suggestion:

Garnish with chopped avocado, sour cream, or salsa.

Variation:

Add steamed and cut-up shrimp, fried and crumbled bacon, or fully cooked, cubed or chipped ham to Step 2.

Grits Casserole

Sue Williams, Gulfport, MS

Makes 6 servings

Prep. Time: 15 minutes ❧ *Baking Time: 15–20 minutes*

1 cup quick-cooking grits
4 cups water
1 tsp. salt
8 Tbsp. (1 stick) butter
¼ lb. sharp cheddar cheese, grated
2 eggs, beaten

1. Cook grits in boiling, salted water for 5 minutes. Add butter and cheese. Stir until well mixed. Cool.
2. Add beaten eggs and mix thoroughly.
3. Pour mixture into a greased pan or casserole dish.
4. Bake at 400°F for 15–20 minutes, or until lightly browned.
5. Serve hot.

Appetizers & Snacks

Puppy Chow

Lena Sheaffer, Port Matilda, PA

Makes 15 servings

Prep. Time: 20 minutes ❧ *Cooking Time: 5–7 minutes*

8 Tbsp. (1 stick) butter

1 cup peanut butter

1 cup chocolate chips

9 cups cereal (Chex, Cheerios, or a mixture)

2 cups confectioners' sugar

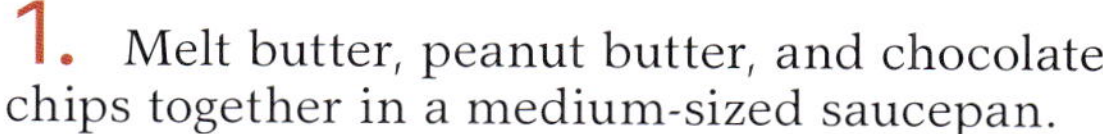

1. Melt butter, peanut butter, and chocolate chips together in a medium-sized saucepan.

2. Place cereal in a large bowl. Pour sauce over cereal, stirring it in as you pour to make sure cereal is well coated.

3. When cereal is cool, put cereal and confectioners' sugar in a ziplock bag.

4. Make sure bag is securely locked. Coat cereal evenly by shaking it together with the sugar.

5. Store in airtight container or ziplock bags.

Deviled Eggs

Leona Yoder, Hartville, OH

Makes 8 servings

Cooking Time: 15–20 minutes *Prep. Time: 10 minutes*

- 4 eggs
- ⅛ tsp. salt
- 2 tsp. vinegar
- 1 Tbsp. mayonnaise
- ⅛ tsp. pepper
- ¼ tsp. prepared mustard
- 1 Tbsp. cream or milk
- ¼ cup finely chopped red onions
- Paprika or fresh parsley leaves

1. Place eggs in a saucepan. Cover with water. Cover pan and bring water to boil.

2. Remove pan with eggs from heat. Keep covered and allow eggs to sit in hot water for 15 minutes. Remove eggs from pan and allow to cool. Peel carefully.

3. Cut eggs in half lengthwise. Remove yolks and place in a small bowl. Mash until smooth.

4. Add remaining ingredients to mashed yolks and mix well.

5. Refill the whites with yolk mixture and garnish with paprika or parsley just before serving.

Tips:

- You can use this recipe as the filling for egg salad sandwiches. Simply cut up the hard-boiled eggs (whites and yolks) and mix gently with the other ingredients.
  —Leona Yoder, Hartville, OH

- I find the Instant Pot the most reliable way for making hard-boiled eggs. Place 1 cup of water in the bottom of the Instant Pot. Place the 4 eggs on a trivet. Secure the lid and set the vent to sealing. Manually set the cook time for 5 minutes. When cook time is up, let the pressure come down naturally for 5 minutes, then manually release the remaining pressure. Place the eggs immediately into an ice bath. Peel them when they are cool.
  —Hope Comerford, Clinton Township, MI

Barbecued Cocktail Sausages

Jena Hammond, Traverse City, MI

Makes 48–60 appetizer servings

Prep. Time: 5 minutes ∘ *Cooking Time: 4 hours* ∘ *Ideal slow-cooker size: 4-qt.*

4 (16-oz.) pkg. little smoked cocktail sausages

18-oz. bottle barbecue sauce

1. Mix ingredients together in slow cooker.
2. Cover and cook on Low for 4 hours.

Honey Barbecue Meatballs

Hope Comerford, Clinton Township, MI

Makes 15–20 servings

Prep. Time: 15 minutes ⁂ *Cooking Time: 4 hours, 15 minutes* ⁂ *Ideal slow-cooker size: 3–4 qt.*

Meatballs:

1 lb. lean ground beef
1 egg
¾ cup panko breadcrumbs
2 Tbsp. minced dry onion
1 Tbsp. garlic powder
1 tsp. salt
¼ tsp. pepper
2–3 Tbsp. olive oil

Sauce:

1 cup barbecue sauce
¼ cup honey
2 tsp. Worcestershire sauce
½ tsp. salt
⅛ tsp. pepper

1. Mix the meatball ingredients (except the oil) together and form into small meatballs.

2. In a large skillet, heat the olive oil over medium-high heat. Brown the meatballs lightly, just until they are sealed on all sides.

3. Place the meatballs into the crock.

4. In a bowl, mix the sauce ingredients. Pour over the meatballs.

5. Cover and cook on Low for 4 hours.

Texas Caviar

Reita F. Yoder, Carlsbad, NM

Makes about 8 cups, or about 20 appetizer-sized servings

Prep. Time: 20 minutes · *Cooling Time: Overnight*

2 (15-oz.) cans black-eyed peas, drained
15-oz. can white hominy, drained
1 medium onion, chopped
2 jalapeño peppers, minced
2 cloves garlic, minced
½ tsp. black pepper
¼ cup minced parsley
1 large tomato, chopped
8-oz. bottle Italian salad dressing

1. Combine all ingredients and refrigerate overnight.
2. Drain before serving.

Serving suggestion:
Serve with corn chips.

Hot Virginia Dip

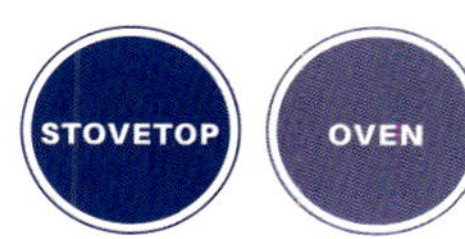

Sue Suter, Millersville, PA

Makes 4 cups

Prep. Time: 20–30 minutes *Baking Time: 20–25 minutes*

1 cup chopped pecans
2 Tbsp. butter
2 (8-oz.) pkg. cream cheese, softened
4 Tbsp. milk
5 oz. dried beef, chopped
1 tsp. garlic powder
1 cup sour cream
4 tsp. chopped onion

1. In skillet, sauté pecans in butter. Set aside.
2. Combine remaining ingredients. Spread in greased baking dish.
3. Sprinkle sautéed pecans over top.
4. Bake at 350°F for 20–25 minutes.

Cheesy Shrimp New Orleans Shrimp Dip

Kelly Amos, Pittsboro, NC

Makes 3–4 cups dip, or 24 servings

Prep. Time: 20–30 minutes · *Cooking Time: 1 hour* · *Ideal slow-cooker size: 2-qt.*

- 1 slice lean turkey bacon
- 3 medium-sized onions, chopped
- 1 clove garlic, minced
- 4 jumbo shrimp, peeled and deveined
- 1 medium-sized tomato, peeled and chopped
- 3 cups shredded low-fat Monterey Jack cheese
- 4 drops Tabasco sauce
- ⅛ tsp. cayenne pepper
- Dash black pepper

1. Cook bacon until crisp. Drain on paper towel. Cut fine.
2. Sauté onions and garlic in bacon drippings. Drain on paper towel.
3. Coarsely chop shrimp.
4. Combine all ingredients in slow cooker.
5. Cover. Cook on Low 1 hour, or until cheese is melted. Thin with milk if too thick.

Serving suggestion:

Serve with chips.

Buffalo Chicken Dip

Deb Martin, Gap, PA

Makes 8 cups

Prep. Time: 15 minutes ⁂ *Cooking Time: 20–60 minutes*

10-oz. can chunk chicken, drained

1/4 cup Frank's RedHot Original Cayenne Pepper Sauce

2 (8-oz.) pkg. cream cheese, softened

1 cup ranch dressing

1 1/2–3 cups shredded cheddar jack cheese, *divided*

Tortilla chips

1. Heat chicken and hot sauce in a large frying pan over medium heat until heated through.
2. Stir in cream cheese and ranch dressing. Cook, stirring until well blended and warm.
3. Mix in half of shredded cheese.
4. Transfer the mixture to a small slow cooker. Sprinkle the remaining cheese over the top.
5. Cover and cook on Low setting until hot and bubbly. Serve with tortilla chips.

Variation:

Replace the hot sauce with 1 cup buffalo wing sauce. Spread cream cheese on the bottom of a small shallow baking dish. Layer with shredded chicken, buffalo wing sauce, ranch dressing, and shredded cheese. Bake at 350°F for 20 minutes or until cheese is melted.

—Donna Treloar, Muncie, IN

Easy Layered Taco Dip

Lindsey Spencer, Morrow, OH
Jenny R. Unternahrer, Wayland, IA

Makes 8–10 servings

Prep. Time: 15 minutes

8-oz. cream cheese, softened
8-oz. sour cream
8-oz. taco sauce or salsa
Shredded lettuce
Chopped tomato
Chopped green pepper, *optional*
Shredded cheese, cheddar or Mexican blend
Tortilla chips

1. Blend cream cheese and sour cream until smooth.
2. Spread in bottom of a 9 × 13-inch dish.
3. Layer salsa over sour cream mixture, then lettuce, tomato, green pepper (if using), and cheese.
4. Serve with tortilla chips.

Variations:

- Instead of salsa, use 1-oz. packet of taco seasoning to mix with the cream cheese and sour cream.
  —Virginia Graybill, Hershey, PA
- Add a layer of chopped onion.
  —Barbara J. Bey, Hillsboro, OH

Tip:

If you can, add the lettuce, tomato, and cheese at the last minute so the lettuce doesn't get soggy.
—Jenny R. Unternahrer, Wayland, IA

Main Dishes

Beef & Lamb

Hoosier Lamb Chops

Willard E. Roth, Elkhart, IN

Makes 6 servings

Prep. Time: 10 minutes ❧ *Cooking Time: 20 minutes*

- 1 Tbsp. oil
- 6 lamb chops
- 1 onion, finely chopped
- 1 Tbsp. balsamic vinegar
- 1 tsp. coarsely ground black pepper
- ¼ cup black currant or black raspberry jam
- ¼ cup red wine
- 1 Tbsp. chopped fresh mint

1. Heat oil in skillet over medium heat. Cook chops, 2 or 3 at a time, for 2 minutes per side until browned. Set aside. Reserve drippings.

2. Sauté onion for 1 minute in same skillet. Add vinegar, pepper, jam, and wine to skillet. Cook until thickened. Stir in fresh mint.

3. Return chops to skillet. Cook 2–3 minutes per side, or until just done. Adjust seasoning. Serve.

Serving suggestion:

This would be great served with a nice salad and Oven Fries on page 142.

Smoky Brisket

Angeline Lang, Greeley, CO

Makes 8–10 servings

Prep. Time: 5 minutes ❧ *Cooking Time: 10–12 hours* ❧ *Ideal slow-cooker size: 4½- or 5-qt.*

- 2 medium onions, sliced
- 3–4-lb. beef brisket
- 1 Tbsp. smoke-flavored salt
- 1 tsp. celery seed
- 1 Tbsp. mustard seed
- ½ tsp. pepper
- 12-oz. bottle chili sauce

1. Arrange onions in bottom of slow cooker.
2. Sprinkle both sides of meat with smoke-flavored salt.
3. Combine celery seed, mustard seed, pepper, and chili sauce. Pour over meat.
4. Cover. Cook on Low 10–12 hours.

Serving suggestion:

This would be great served with Easy Red Potato Salad on page 158 or Slow-Cooked Baked Beans on page 146.

Hearty Pot Roast

Colleen Heatwole, Burton, MI

Makes 12 servings, about 1 cup per serving

Prep. Time: 30 minutes ❧ *Roasting Time: 2–2½ hours* ❧ *Standing Time: 10 minutes*

- 4-lb. beef roast, ideally rump roast
- 4 medium red potatoes, cut in thirds
- 3 medium carrots, quartered
- 2 ribs celery, chopped
- 2 medium onions, sliced
- ½ cup flour
- 6-oz. can tomato paste
- ¼ cup water
- 1 tsp. instant beef bouillon, or 1 beef bouillon cube
- ¼ tsp. pepper

1. Place roast in 9 × 13-inch baking pan or roaster.
2. Arrange vegetables around roast.
3. Combine flour, tomato paste, water, bouillon, and pepper in small bowl.
4. Pour over meat and vegetables.
5. Cover. Roast at 325°F for 2–2½ hours, or until meat thermometer registers 170°F.
6. Allow meat to stand for 10 minutes.
7. Slice and place on platter surrounded by vegetables.
8. Pour gravy over top. Place additional gravy in bowl and serve along with platter.

Variation:

You can make this in a large oven cooking bag. Combine flour, tomato paste, water, bouillon, and pepper in a bowl. Pour into cooking bag. Place in 9 × 13-inch baking pan. Add roast to bag in pan. Add vegetables around roast in bag. Close bag with its tie. Make six 1/2-inch slits on top of bag. Roast according to instructions in Step 5 and following.

Deep, Dark & Delicious Barbecue Sandwiches

Phyllis Good, Lancaster, PA

Makes 14–18 servings

Prep. Time: 20–30 minutes (use a food chopper) ✿ *Cooking Time: 5–10 hours*
Ideal slow-cooker size: 5-qt.

- 3 cups chopped celery
- 1 cup chopped onions
- 1 cup ketchup
- 1 cup barbecue sauce
- 1 cup water
- 2 Tbsp. vinegar
- 2 Tbsp. Worcestershire sauce
- ¼ cup dark brown sugar
- 1 tsp. salt
- ½ tsp. pepper
- 3–4-lb. boneless chuck roast
- 14–18 hamburger buns

1. Combine all ingredients except roast and buns in slow cooker. When well mixed, put the roast in the cooker. Spoon sauce over top of it.

2. Cover. Cook on High 5–6 hours, or on Low 8–10 hours.

3. Using two forks, pull the meat apart until it's shredded. You can do this in the cooker, or lift it out and do it on a good-sized platter or in a bowl.

4. Stir shredded meat into sauce. Turn the cooker to High if you're ready to eat soon. Or if it will be a while until mealtime, turn the cooker to Low. You're just making sure that the meat and sauce are heated through completely.

5. Serve on buns.

Serving suggestion:

These would be great served with Best-in-the-West Beans on page 143 and Macaroni Salad on page 150.

Walking Tacos

Hope Comerford, Clinton Township, MI

Makes 10–16 servings

Prep. Time: 10 minutes ❧ *Cooking Time: 6–7 hours* ❧ *Ideal slow-cooker size: 2–3 qt.*

2 lb. ground beef
2 tsp. garlic powder
2 tsp. onion powder
1 Tbsp. cumin
2 Tbsp. chili powder
1 tsp. salt
½ tsp. oregano
½ tsp. red pepper flakes
1 small onion, minced
1 clove garlic, minced
10–16 individual-sized bags of Doritos or Fritos

Suggested toppings:
Diced tomatoes
Shredded cheese
Diced cucumbers
Chopped onion,
Shredded lettuce
Sour cream
Salsa

1. Crumble the ground beef into the crock.
2. In a bowl, mix all the spices, onion, and garlic. Pour this over beef, then stir it up.
3. Cover and cook for 6–7 hours, breaking it up occasionally.
4. Remove some of the grease if you wish.
5. To serve, open a bag of Doritos, crumble the chips in the bag with your hand, add some of the ground beef to the bag, then any additional toppings you desire. Serve each bag with a fork.

Taco Meatloaf

Tammy Smith, Dorchester, WI

Makes 8 servings

Prep. Time: 20 minutes · *Cooking Time: 4 hours* · *Ideal slow-cooker size: oval 5- or 6-qt.*

3 eggs, lightly beaten
½ cup crushed tomatoes
¾ cup crushed tortilla chips
1 medium onion, finely chopped
2 cloves garlic, minced
3 tsp. taco seasoning
2 tsp. chili powder
1 lb. ground beef
1 lb. ground pork
½ tsp. salt
¾ tsp. black pepper

Serving suggestion:
This would be great served with Corn on the Cob on page 134.

1. Grease interior of slow-cooker crock.
2. Make a tinfoil sling for your slow cooker so you can lift the cooked meatloaf out easily. Begin by folding a strip of foil accordion-fashion so that it's about 1½–2 inches wide, and long enough to fit from the top edge of the crock, down inside and up the other side, plus a 2-inch overhang on each side of the cooker. Make a second strip exactly like the first.
3. Place one strip in crock, running from end to end. Place second strip in crock, running from side to side. The strips should form a cross in bottom of the crock.
4. In a large bowl, combine all ingredients well.
5. Shape into a loaf. Place into crock so that the center of loaf sits where the two strips of foil cross.
6. Cover. Cook for 4 hours on Low.
7. Using the foil handles, lift loaf onto platter. Cover to keep warm. Let stand for 10–15 minutes before slicing.

Beef and Pepperoncini Hoagies

Donna Treloar, Muncie, IN

Makes 10 servings (varies with roast size)

Prep. Time: 15 minutes ♣ *Cooking Time: 8–10 hours* ♣ *Ideal slow-cooker size: 5- or 6-qt.*

3–5-lb. boneless chuck roast (inexpensive cuts work fine)

Salt to taste

Pepper to taste

1 clove garlic, minced, or 1 tsp. garlic powder

16-oz. jar of pepperoncini peppers, mild or medium, depending on your preference

Hoagie rolls or buns of your choice

20 slices provolone cheese

1. Grease interior of slow-cooker crock.
2. Trim fat off roast.
3. Salt and pepper, to taste, holding over crock.
4. If using garlic powder, sprinkle on all sides of beef over crock. Place beef in crock.
5. If using minced garlic, scatter over beef in crock.
6. If the pepperoncini peppers are whole and have stems, remove peppers from jar and cut up. Reserve liquid.
7. Scatter cut-up peppers over meat.
8. Pour liquid from peppers down alongside of crock interior so you don't wash off the seasonings.
9. Cover. Cook on Low 7½–9½ hours, or until beef registers 160°F on an instant-read meat thermometer when stuck in center of roast.
10. Lift roast into a big bowl and shred with two forks.
11. Stir shredded meat back into juices in crock.
12. Cover. Cook another 30 minutes on Low.
13. When ready to serve, use a slotted spoon to drain meat well.
14. Spoon well-drained meat onto a hoagie roll and top each sandwich with 2 slices cheese.

Variation

You can add chopped onions to Step 7 and/or a package of dry Italian dressing mix or Lipton Onion Soup Mix and a cup or two of beef broth to Steps 7 and 8.

Serving suggestion:

This goes well with sweet potato fries.

Philly Cheesesteaks

Michele Ruvola, Vestal, NY

Makes 6 servings

Prep. Time: 15 minutes *Cooking Time: 11 minutes*

1 red pepper, sliced
1 green pepper, sliced
1 onion, sliced
2 cloves garlic, minced
2½ lb. thinly sliced steak
1 tsp. salt
½ tsp. black pepper
0.7-oz. pkg. dry Italian dressing mix
1 cup water
1 beef bouillon cube
6 slices provolone cheese
6 hoagie rolls

1. Put all ingredients in the inner pot of the Instant Pot, except the provolone cheese and rolls.
2. Seal the lid, make sure vent is at sealing. Manually set the cook for 6 minutes on high pressure.
3. When cook time is up, let the pressure release naturally for 10 minutes, then manually release the remaining pressure.
4. Scoop meat and vegetables into rolls.
5. Top with provolone cheese and put on a baking sheet.
6. Broil in oven for 5 minutes.
7. Pour remaining juice in pot into cups for dipping.

So-Good Sloppy Joes

Judy Diller, Bluffton, OH

Makes 18 servings

Prep. Time: 20 minutes ❧ *Cooking Time: 4–5 hours* ❧ *Ideal slow-cooker size: 5- or 6-qt.*

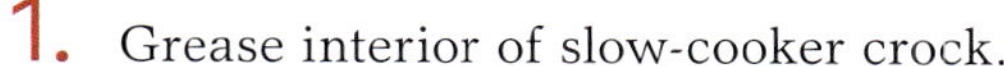

- 3 lb. ground beef
- 1 medium onion, chopped
- 1 green bell pepper, diced
- 10¾-oz. can tomato soup
- 1 cup ketchup (use a lively one if you like some kick)
- 2 Tbsp. prepared mustard (use a spicy variety if you want some extra zest)
- 2 Tbsp. apple cider vinegar
- 1 Tbsp. brown sugar
- 2 Tbsp. Worcestershire sauce
- 18 burger buns

1. Grease interior of slow-cooker crock.
2. If you have time, brown beef in large skillet. Using a slotted spoon, lift beef out of drippings and place in crock. If you don't have time, place beef in crock and use a sturdy spoon to break it up into small clumps.
3. Stir in all remaining ingredients except rolls.
4. Cover. Cook on Low 4–5 hours, or until beef is fully cooked and veggies are as tender as you like them.
5. Serve in buns. Turn the cooker to Warm and serve the So-Good Sloppy Joes over a several-hour period if you wish.

Serving suggestion:

These would go great with Barbecued Green Beans on page 141 and Potato Salad on page 157.

Grilled Burgers

Deborah Heatwole, Waynesboro, GA

Makes 12 servings

Prep. Time: 10–15 minutes ❀ *Grilling Time: 10–15 minutes*

2 lb. ground beef
¾ cup uncooked rolled, or quick, oats
2 eggs
⅓ cup ketchup
1½ tsp. dried onion, *optional*
1 tsp. Worcestershire sauce, *optional*
Salt to taste
Pepper to taste

1. Mix ground beef thoroughly with the rest of the ingredients.
2. Shape ⅓ cupfuls into patties.
3. Place patties on hot grill. Grill, covered, 5–7 minutes per side, or until centers of burgers are no longer pink.

Serving suggestions:

- Serve on buns with toppings of your choice.
- These would go great with Grilled Vegetables on page 136 and Creamy Dill Pasta Salad on page 151.

Cheeseburger Casserole

STOVETOP OVEN

Sherri Mayer, Menomonee Falls, WI

Makes 4 servings

Prep. Time: 15–20 minutes ⁂ *Cooking/Baking Time: 35–40 minutes*

- 1 lb. ground beef
- ½ cup chopped onions
- ¼ cup chopped green pepper
- 8-oz. can tomato sauce
- ¼ cup ketchup
- ⅛ tsp. pepper
- ½ lb. sliced American cheese, or your choice of cheese
- 4-oz. can refrigerated biscuits

1. In a large skillet, brown ground beef with onions and green pepper. Drain off drippings.
2. Blend in tomato sauce, ketchup, and pepper. Cook on low heat about 5 minutes.
3. In greased 2-qt. casserole dish, alternate layers of ground beef mixture and slices of cheese.
4. Arrange biscuits on top.
5. Bake at 400°F 20–25 minutes, until biscuits are golden brown.

Reuben Casserole

Joleen Albrecht, Gladstone, MI

Makes 8–10 servings

Prep. Time: 25 minutes · *Baking Time: 25 minutes*

1½ cups Thousand Island salad dressing
1 cup sour cream
1 Tbsp. minced onions
12 slices dark rye bread, cubed, *divided*
1 lb. sauerkraut, drained
1½ lb. corned beef, sliced and cut into bite-sized pieces
2 cups shredded Swiss cheese
¼ cup melted butter or margarine

1. In a mixing bowl, stir together dressing, sour cream, and onions. Set aside.
2. Arrange bread cubes in a greased 9 × 13-inch baking dish, setting aside approximately 1 cup cubes for the top.
3. Top the bread with a layer of sauerkraut, followed by a layer of corned beef.
4. Spread dressing mixture over corned beef. Sprinkle with Swiss cheese.
5. Top with remaining bread cubes. Drizzle with melted butter.
6. Cover and bake at 350°F for 15 minutes. Uncover and continue baking for about 10 minutes or until bubbly.

Serving suggestion:

This would go great with Broccoli Slaw on page 160.

Texas Cottage Pie

Kathy Hertzler, Lancaster, PA

Makes 6 servings

Prep. Time: 25–30 minutes ❀ *Baking Time: 30–35 minutes*

- 1 Tbsp. oil
- 1 medium onion, diced
- 1 lb. lean ground beef
- ½ tsp. salt
- ½ tsp. cumin
- ½ tsp. paprika
- 1 tsp. chili powder
- ¼ tsp. black pepper
- ¼ tsp. cinnamon
- 1 tsp. chopped garlic
- 15-oz. can black beans, rinsed and drained
- 1 cup frozen corn
- 14½-oz. can diced tomatoes with green chilies
- 3 cups leftover mashed potatoes
- ½ cup milk
- 1 cup shredded pepper jack cheese, *divided*

1. In large skillet, sauté diced onion and ground beef in 1 Tbsp. oil until beef is almost cooked through. Stir frequently to break up clumps of meat. Drain off any drippings.
2. Add salt, spices, seasonings, and garlic to skillet.
3. Cook 2 minutes more on medium heat.
4. Add black beans, corn, and tomatoes with chilies. Stir well.
5. Cover. Cook on low heat 15 minutes.
6. Meanwhile, warm mashed potatoes mixed with ½ cup milk in microwaveable bowl in microwave (2 minutes, covered, on Power 8), or in saucepan on stove top (covered and over very low heat for 5–10 minutes, stirring frequently to prevent sticking).
7. Stir ½ cup cheese into warmed mashed potatoes.
8. Transfer meat mixture to greased 7 × 10-inch baking dish.
9. Top with mashed potatoes, spreading in an even layer to edges of baking dish.
10. Sprinkle with the remaining ½ cup cheese.
11. Bake at 350°F for 30–35 minutes.

(Continued)

Tip:

The amounts in this recipe are flexible. For example, the original recipe called for only 1 cup of black beans and 1 cup of tomatoes. You can use more cheese and more mashed potatoes. It's a very forgiving recipe. Adjust it to accommodate whatever you have on hand, and the people you'll be feeding.

Serving suggestion:

This goes well with a tossed green salad and Sour Cream Cornbread on page 168.

Connecticut Supper

Virginia Graybill, Hershey, PA

Makes 8 servings

Prep. Time: 30–40 minutes ♣ *Baking Time: 1½ hours*

- 2 lb. hamburger
- ½ cup chopped onions
- 5 or 6 medium-sized potatoes
- 10¾-oz. can cream of mushroom soup
- 1 cup sour cream
- 1¼ cups milk
- 1½ cups shredded cheddar cheese
- 1 tsp. salt
- ¼ tsp. pepper

1. Cook hamburger and onions in nonstick skillet, stirring frequently to break up clumps of meat. Continue cooking until no pink remains in meat. Drain off any drippings.
2. Place browned meat and onions in bottom of greased 9 × 13-inch baking dish.
3. Peel and thinly slice potatoes. Distribute over top of meat.
4. In a good-sized mixing bowl, blend together soup, sour cream, and milk until smooth.
5. Stir cheese, salt, and pepper into creamy sauce.
6. Pour over potatoes.
7. Bake at 350°F for 1½ hours, or until potatoes are completely tender when poked with a fork.

Pork

Barbecued Pork Ribs

Michele Ruvola, Vestal, NY

Makes 8 servings

Prep. Time: 5 minutes ❧ *Cooking Time: 9–10 hours* ❧ *Ideal slow-cooker size: 4-qt.*

- 2 Tbsp. dried minced onion
- 1 tsp. crushed red pepper
- ½ tsp. ground cinnamon
- ½ tsp. garlic powder
- 3 lb. pork loin back ribs, cut into serving-sized pieces
- 1 medium onion, sliced
- ½ cup water
- 1½ cups barbecue sauce

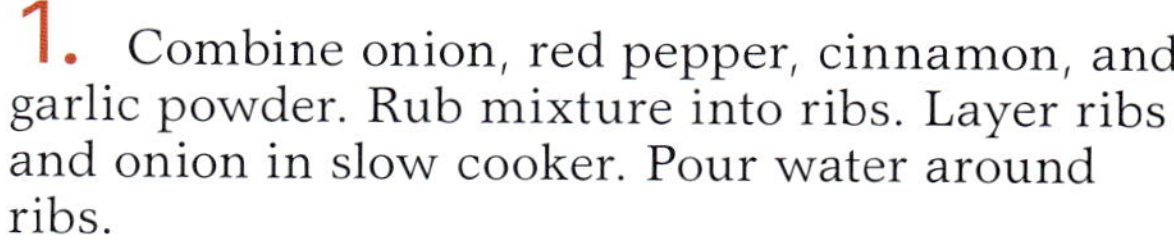

1. Combine onion, red pepper, cinnamon, and garlic powder. Rub mixture into ribs. Layer ribs and onion in slow cooker. Pour water around ribs.

2. Cover. Cook on Low 8–9 hours.

3. Remove ribs from slow cooker. Drain and discard liquid. Pour barbecue sauce in bowl and dip ribs in sauce. Return ribs to slow cooker. Pour remaining sauce over ribs.

4. Cover. Cook on Low 1 hour.

Serving suggestion:

These would go great with Aunt Mary's Baked Corn on page 133.

Finger-Lickin' Spareribs

Susan Guarneri, Three Lakes, WI

Makes 4 servings

Prep. Time: 25 minutes ❧ *Cooking Time: 1 hour 25 minutes*

- 2 lb. spareribs, cut in pieces
- ¼ cup oil
- ¼ cup chopped onions
- ¼ cup chopped green pepper
- 1 cup pineapple juice
- ¾ cup vinegar
- ¾ cup water
- 2 Tbsp. ketchup
- 1 Tbsp. soy sauce
- ¼ tsp. Worcestershire sauce
- 1 medium clove garlic, minced
- ½ cup brown sugar
- 2 Tbsp. cornstarch

1. Brown spareribs in oil in large skillet. Remove meat and pour off all but 2 Tbsp. drippings.

2. Add onions and green pepper to drippings and cook until tender. Stir in juice, vinegar, water, ketchup, soy sauce, Worcestershire sauce, and garlic. Bring to boil.

3. Blend brown sugar and cornstarch together and quickly stir into boiling mixture until thickened (a minute or two).

4. Reduce heat to low simmer and add meat. Cook uncovered for 1 hour, or until tender. Stir occasionally so the sauce and meat do not burn. Check meat from time to time—it may take less than an hour to cook to fork-tender.

Serving suggestion:

These would go great with Absolutely Creamy Spinach on page 138.

Variation:

Add 1 cup pineapple chunks plus 1 cup juice for a heartier dish.

Pulled Pork

Janet Batdorf, Harrisburg, PA

Makes 10 servings

Prep. Time: 20 minutes ❧ *Cooking Time: 9 hours*
Chilling Time for broth: 4–5 hours ❧ *Ideal slow-cooker size: 5-qt.*

3-lb. pork roast

Sauce:

1 cup ketchup
1 cup pork broth
2 Tbsp. Worcestershire sauce
2 Tbsp. vinegar
Dash pepper
¾ tsp. salt
2 Tbsp. prepared mustard
1 large onion, chopped

1. Place pork in slow cooker.
2. Cover with water.
3. Cover. Cook overnight, or for approximately 8 hours, on Low.
4. Turn off slow cooker.
5. Remove pork and set aside.
6. Refrigerate broth.
7. Skim off fat when cold.
8. Combine sauce ingredients in slow cooker.
9. Shred pork with two forks.
10. Add shredded pork to sauce.
11. Turn slow cooker on Low. Heat pork in sauce for about one hour, or until ingredients are hot and bubbly.

Serving suggestions:

- Serve in buns, or over mashed potatoes, rice, or pasta.
- This would go great with Collard Greens with Bacon on page 139.

Smoked Barbecue Pork Sandwiches

Hope Comerford, Clinton Township, MI

Makes 8 servings

Prep. Time: 15–20 minutes ✿ *Refrigeration Time: 8 hours*
Cooking Time: 8 hours ✿ *Ideal slow-cooker size: 4-qt.*

- 3–4-lb. boneless pork loin roast
- ⅛ tsp. celery salt
- ¼ tsp. garlic salt
- ¼ tsp. onion salt
- ¼ tsp. salt
- 3 Tbsp. liquid smoke
- 1½ cups barbecue sauce
- 8 hamburger buns

1. Place pork roast in slow-cooker crock.
2. Sprinkle with celery salt, garlic salt, onion salt, and salt.
3. Pour liquid smoke over the roast. Cover. Refrigerate for 8 hours.
4. Cook on Low 8 hours, or until tender. During last hour, pour barbecue sauce over roast.
5. Pull meat apart and mix in sauce. Serve on hamburger buns.

Serving suggestion:

This would go great with American Beans on page 144.

Chops and Beans

Mary L. Casey, Scranton, PA

Makes 4–6 servings

Prep. Time: 15–20 minutes ✤ *Cooking Time: 4–6 hours* ✤ *Ideal slow-cooker size: 4-qt.*

2 (1-lb.) cans pork and beans
½ cup ketchup
2 slices bacon, browned and crumbled
½ cup chopped onions, sautéed
1 Tbsp. Worcestershire sauce
¼ cup firmly packed brown sugar
4–6 pork chops
2 tsp. prepared mustard
1 Tbsp. brown sugar
¼ cup ketchup
1 lemon, sliced

1. Combine beans, ½ cup ketchup, bacon, onions, Worcestershire sauce, and ¼ cup brown sugar in slow cooker.

2. Brown chops in skillet. In separate bowl, mix the 2 tsp. mustard, 1 Tbsp. brown sugar, and ¼ cup ketchup. Brush each chop with sauce, then carefully stack into cooker, placing a slice of lemon on each chop. Submerge in bean/bacon mixture.

3. Cover. Cook on Low 4–6 hours.

Baked Pork Chops with Gravy

Margaret Jarrett, Anderson, IN

Makes 4 servings

Prep. Time: 15 minutes ⁂ *Cooking/Baking Time: 75 minutes*

1 Tbsp. oil
4 pork chops
10¾-oz. can cream of mushroom soup
¾ cup water
½ tsp. ground ginger
¼ tsp. rosemary
1 can onion rings
¼ cup sour cream

1. Brown pork chops in oil in skillet. (Reserve the drippings.) Lay the browned chops in a lightly greased baking dish.

2. In a small mixing bowl, mix the mushroom soup, water, ginger, and rosemary together. Pour over the chops.

3. Cover and bake at 350°F for 50 minutes.

4. Uncover and spread onion rings over top. Bake 10 more minutes.

5. While the chops are baking, make a gravy by heating the drippings. Stir in the sour cream and heat without boiling. Serve with the baked chops.

Serving suggestion:
These would go great with Marge's Cauliflower on page 135.

Tomato-Glazed Pork with Grilled Corn Salsa

Janet Melvin, Cincinnati, OH

Makes 6–8 servings

Prep. Time: 45 minutes ❧ *Cooking Time: 3–4 hours* ❧ *Ideal slow-cooker size: 5-qt.*

Tomato glaze:

2 Tbsp. dry mustard
1 Tbsp. ground ginger
1 Tbsp. ground fennel
1 Tbsp. minced garlic
¼ cup mayonnaise
1 cup ketchup
¼ cup honey
1 Tbsp. Worcestershire sauce
¼ cup grated fresh horseradish
3 Tbsp. white wine mustard
2 Tbsp. minced capers
1 Tbsp. Tabasco sauce
2-lb. boneless pork loin roast, short and wide in shape

Salsa:

3 ears sweet corn, husked and silked, or 4 cups frozen or canned corn
½ cup olive oil
¼ cup chopped sun-dried tomatoes
1 clove garlic, minced
½ cup wild mushrooms, sliced
2 Tbsp. chopped fresh cilantro
2 Tbsp. fresh lime juice
1 chipotle pepper in adobo sauce, finely chopped
½ tsp. salt

1. Grease interior of slow-cooker crock.
2. Prepare glaze by mixing the dry mustard, ginger, fennel, garlic, and mayonnaise.
3. When well blended, stir in remaining glaze ingredients.
4. Place pork in slow cooker, fat side up. Cover with glaze.
5. Cover. Cook on Low 3–4 hours, or until instant-read meat thermometer registers 140°F when stuck into center of roast.
6. While roast is cooking, brush ears of corn with olive oil. Wrap in foil.
7. Bake at 350°F for 15 minutes. Unwrap and grill or broil until evenly browned.
8. Cool. Cut kernels from cob.
9. Combine corn with rest of salsa ingredients.
10. Cover and refrigerate until ready to use.
11. When pork is finished cooking, remove from cooker to cutting board. Cover with foil and let stand for 10 minutes.
12. Slice and serve on top of grilled corn salsa.

Jiffy Jambalaya

Carole M. Mackie, Williamsfield, IL

Makes 6 servings

Prep. Time: 30 minutes · *Cooking Time: 10–15 minutes*

- 1 onion, chopped
- ½ cup chopped green pepper
- 2 Tbsp. oil
- 1 lb. cooked kielbasa or Polish sausage, cut into ¼-inch slices
- 28-oz. can diced tomatoes, undrained
- ½ cup water
- 1 Tbsp. sugar
- 1 tsp. paprika
- ½ tsp. dried thyme
- ½ tsp. dried oregano
- ¼ tsp. garlic powder
- 3 drops hot pepper sauce
- 1½ cups uncooked instant rice

1. In skillet, sauté onion and green pepper in oil until tender.

2. Stir in sausage, tomatoes, water, sugar, and seasonings. Bring to a boil.

3. Add rice. Cover and simmer for 5 minutes, until rice is tender.

Ham Loaf

Inez Rutt, Bangor, PA

Makes 6–8 servings

Prep. Time: 20–30 minutes · *Baking Time: 1–1¼ hours*

¾ lb. ground ham
¾ lb. ground pork
1 egg
¼ cup minced onions
½ cup cracker crumbs
½ cup milk
Pepper to taste

Glaze:

½ cup brown sugar
1 Tbsp. dry mustard
¼ cup vinegar

1. In a large mixing bowl, mix ham, pork, egg, onions, cracker crumbs, milk, and pepper together until well blended. Form into a loaf then place in a greased loaf pan.

2. Make glaze by mixing brown sugar, dry mustard, and vinegar together until smooth.

3. Pour glaze over top of ham loaf.

4. Bake at 350°F for 1–1¼ hours, or until well browned. Baste occasionally with glaze during baking.

Serving suggestion:

This would go great with Spring Pea Salad on page 155.

Variation:

Add 8-oz. can crushed pineapple and juice to the glaze.

—Mary E. Wheatley, Mashpee, MA
—Janice Yoskovich, Carmichaels, PA

Chicken

Crispy Chicken

Kitty Hilliard, Punxsutawney, PA

Makes 4 servings

Prep. Time: 10 minutes · *Baking Time: 20–25 minutes*

- 2 Tbsp. flour
- 1½ cups crisp rice cereal, coarsely crushed
- ½ tsp. salt
- ¼ tsp. dried thyme
- ¼ tsp. poultry seasoning
- 4 Tbsp. (½ stick) butter, melted
- 4 boneless, skinless chicken breast halves, each about 4–6 oz.

1. Grease a 7 × 11-inch baking dish.
2. In a shallow bowl, combine flour, cereal, salt, thyme, and poultry seasoning.
3. Place butter in another shallow bowl.
4. Dip chicken in butter, then into cereal mixture.
5. Place in greased baking pan.
6. Drizzle with remaining butter.
7. Bake at 400°F for 20–25 minutes, or until thermometer inserted in center registers 165°F.

Serving suggestion:

This would go great served with Creamy Dill Pasta Salad on page 151.

Tip:

You can also put the dry ingredients in a storage bag, then drop chicken pieces in and shake to coat.

Baked Chicken Fingers

Lori Rohrer, Washington Boro, PA

Makes 6 servings

Prep. Time: 20 minutes ❧ *Baking Time: 20 minutes*

- 1½ cups fine, dry breadcrumbs
- ½ cup grated Parmesan cheese
- 1½ tsp. salt
- 1 Tbsp. dried thyme
- 1 Tbsp. dried basil
- ½ cup melted butter
- 7 boneless, skinless chicken breast halves, cut into 1½-inch slices

1. Combine breadcrumbs, cheese, salt, and herbs in a shallow bowl. Mix well.
2. Dip chicken pieces in butter, and then into crumb mixture, coating well.
3. Place coated chicken on greased baking sheet in a single layer.
4. Bake at 400°F for 20 minutes.

Serving suggestion:

This would go great served with Spring Pea Salad on page 155.

Variations:

- In Step 1, use 1 Tbsp. garlic powder, 1 Tbsp. chives, 2 tsp. Italian seasoning, 2 tsp. parsley, ½ tsp. onion salt, ½ tsp. pepper, and ¼ tsp. salt (instead of 1½ tsp. salt, 1 Tbsp. thyme, and 1 Tbsp. basil).

  —Ruth Miller, Wooster, OH

- Use boneless, skinless chicken thighs, and do not cut them into slices. Bake at 350°F for 20 minutes. Turn chicken. Bake an additional 20 minutes.

  —Eleanor Larson, Glen Lyon, PA

Oven Barbecued Chicken

Carol Eberly, Harrisonburg, VA

Makes 8–12 servings

Prep. Time: 10 minutes · *Baking Time: 1¼ hours*

- 3 Tbsp. ketchup
- 2 Tbsp. Worcestershire sauce
- 2 Tbsp. vinegar
- 2 Tbsp. soy sauce
- 3 Tbsp. brown sugar
- 1 tsp. spicy brown mustard
- 1 tsp. salt
- 1 tsp. pepper
- 8–12 boneless, skinless chicken thighs

1. In a mixing bowl, combine ketchup, Worcestershire sauce, vinegar, soy sauce, brown sugar, mustard, salt, and pepper. Blend well.
2. Lay chicken pieces in one layer in well-greased baking dish.
3. Pour sauce over top.
4. Bake at 350°F for 40 minutes.
5. Turn pieces over. Bake 35 more minutes.

Serving suggestion:

This would be great served with Slow-Cooked Baked Beans on page 146.

Tip:

You can use chicken legs or chicken breasts, too. Check the legs after they've baked for a total of 50 minutes to be sure they're not drying out. Check breasts after they've baked for a total of 30 minutes to be sure they're not becoming dry.

Barbecued Chicken

Dawn Ranck, Lansdale, PA

Makes 8 servings

Prep. Time: 10 minutes ⁂ Grilling Time: 25–30 minutes

½ cup vinegar
½ Tbsp. salt
8 Tbsp. (1 stick) butter
8 legs and thighs, or 8 whole breasts

Topping:

¼ cup lemon juice
1 Tbsp. brown sugar
1 Tbsp. Worcestershire sauce
1 tsp. salt
½ tsp. dry mustard
8 Tbsp. (1 stick) butter
¾ cup ketchup
2 Tbsp. fresh parsley, chopped
2 Tbsp. fresh, or ¾ tsp. dried, lemon thyme
2 Tbsp. chives, chopped

1. In a small saucepan, combine vinegar, salt, and 1 stick butter. Heat until butter is melted.

2. Grill chicken, brushing frequently with vinegar mixture, until chicken is almost fully cooked.

3. In another saucepan, combine all topping ingredients. Heat until butter is melted. Stir to blend well.

4. Brush topping on chicken. Grill 5 minutes. Turn chicken over. Brush topping on other side and grill an additional 5 minutes.

Serving suggestion:

This would be great served with Corn on the Cob on page 134 and Potato Salad on page 157.

Chicken and Dumplings

Barbara Nolan, Pleasant Valley, NY

Makes 4 servings

Prep. Time: 15 minutes ❧ *Cooking Time: 30 minutes*

- 4 carrots, cut into ½-inch-thick slices
- 2 medium onions, cut into eighths
- 1 clove garlic, sliced thin
- 3 celery ribs, cut into ½-inch-thick slices
- 2 Tbsp. butter
- 3 Tbsp. flour
- 2 (14-oz.) cans chicken broth
- 1 lb. uncooked chicken cutlets, cut into 1-inch cubes
- 2 Tbsp. grated carrots
- ½ tsp. poultry seasoning
- ¼ tsp. garlic powder
- ⅛ tsp. black pepper
- ¼ cup half-and-half
- Fresh parsley

Dumplings:

- 1½ cups flour
- 2 tsp. baking powder
- ¾ tsp. salt
- 1 cup milk
- 1 egg
- 2 Tbsp. vegetable oil

1. Sauté carrot pieces, onions, garlic, and celery in butter in medium sauce pan for 3 minutes, or until vegetables soften.
2. Sprinkle with flour.
3. Stir to combine. Cook 1–2 minutes.
4. Stir in chicken broth, chicken, grated carrots, poultry seasoning, garlic powder, and pepper until smooth.
5. Bring to boil. Simmer 5 minutes, or until thickened, stirring constantly.
6. To prepare dumplings, mix the flour, baking powder, and salt in mixing bowl.
7. In a separate bowl, combine milk, egg, and oil.
8. Add egg-milk mixture to dry ingredients, barely mixing.
9. Drop dumpling batter by tablespoonfuls onto simmering chicken.
10. Cook 10 minutes uncovered.
11. Cover and cook an additional 10 minutes.
12. Pour half-and-half between dumplings into broth.
13. Scatter fresh parsley over top. Serve immediately.

Tip:

Chop all veggies and chicken beforehand and refrigerate until you're ready to make the dish. Doing so makes it very fast to prepare this dish.

Chicken and Biscuits

Hope Comerford, Clinton Township, MI

Makes 4–6 servings

Prep. Time: 5 minutes ❧ *Cooking Time: 6 hours* ❧ *Ideal slow-cooker size: 3-qt.*

- 2 lb. boneless, skinless chicken breasts
- 10½-oz. can condensed cream of chicken soup
- 10½-oz. can condensed cream of potato soup
- ¾ cup milk
- ½ tsp. salt
- ⅛ tsp. pepper
- 2 tsp. garlic powder
- 2 tsp. onion powder
- 1 cup frozen mixed vegetables
- 6 refrigerator biscuits, baked according to the package directions

1. Place the boneless skinless chicken in the crock.
2. In a bowl, mix the cream of chicken soup, cream of potato soup, milk, salt, pepper, garlic powder, onion powder, and frozen mixed vegetables. Pour this over the chicken.
3. Cover and cook on Low for 6 hours.
4. Shred the chicken between two forks and stir back through the contents of the crock.
5. Serve the chicken mixture over the biscuits to serve.

Sizzlin' Chicken Skewers

Cheryl A. Lapp, Parkesburg, PA

Makes 6 servings

Prep. Time: 30 minutes ❧ *Marinating Time: 1½ hours* ❧ *Grilling or Broiling Time: 12 minutes*

- ⅓ cup hot water
- ¼ cup barbecue sauce
- ¼ cup creamy peanut butter
- ¼ cup soy sauce
- 2 Tbsp. honey Dijon mustard
- 1 lb. boneless, skinless chicken breasts, cut into small pieces
- 1 red pepper, cut into chunks
- 1 yellow pepper, cut into chunks
- 2 (15-oz.) cans whole potatoes
- 20-oz. can pineapple chunks
- 1 small zucchini, cut into chunks

1. In a small mixing bowl, combine first five ingredients. Brush small amount onto chicken pieces, enough to cover. Let stand for 1½ hours.

2. Alternate chicken and vegetables and pineapple chunks on skewers and brush with remaining sauce.

3. Place skewers on the grill or under the broiler for approximately 6 minutes. Turn and grill or broil another 6 minutes.

Chicken and Broccoli Bake

Jan Rankin, Millersville, PA

Makes 12–16 servings

Prep. Time: 15 minutes ⁂ *Baking Time: 30 minutes*

- 2 (10¾-oz.) cans cream of chicken soup
- 2½ cups milk, *divided*
- 16-oz. bag frozen chopped broccoli, thawed and drained
- 3 cups cooked, chopped chicken breast
- 2 cups buttermilk baking mix

1. Mix soup and 1 cup milk together in large mixing bowl until smooth.
2. Stir in broccoli and chicken.
3. Pour into well-greased 9 × 13-inch baking dish.
4. Mix together 1½ cups milk and baking mix in mixing bowl.
5. Spoon evenly over top of chicken-broccoli mixture.
6. Bake at 450°F for 30 minutes.

Chicken Monterey

Sally Holzem, Schofield, WI

Makes 4 servings

Prep. Time: 15 minutes ꕥ *Baking Time: 30 minutes*

4 boneless, skinless chicken breast halves, about 1½ lb. total

¼ tsp. salt

⅛ tsp. pepper

⅓ cup bottled barbecue sauce

4–8 slices cooked bacon, according to your taste preference

1 cup shredded cheddar cheese

4 green onions, trimmed and sliced

1 small tomato, chopped

1. Heat oven to 350°F.
2. Place chicken in a single layer in a greased baking dish.
3. Sprinkle with salt and pepper. Spoon on the barbecue sauce.
4. Bake in 350°F oven for 25 minutes, or until all pink is gone.
5. Top each breast half with 1 or 2 slices of cooked bacon. Sprinkle with cheddar cheese.
6. Bake in oven 5 more minutes.
7. Top each breast half with fresh scallions and tomatoes just before serving.

Serving suggestion:

This would be great served with Barbecued Green Beans on page 141.

Heavenly Barbecued Chicken Wings

Tracy Supcoe, Barclay, MD

Makes 8 full-sized servings

Prep. Time: 20 minutes ⁂ *Cooking Time: 5–6 hours* ⁂ *Ideal slow-cooker size: 5-qt.*

- 4 lb. chicken wings
- 2 large onions, chopped
- 2 (6-oz.) cans tomato paste
- 2 large cloves garlic, minced
- ¼ cup Worcestershire sauce
- ¼ cup cider vinegar
- ½ cup brown sugar
- ½ cup sweet pickle relish
- ½ cup red or white wine
- 2 tsp. salt
- 2 tsp. dry mustard

1. Cut off wing tips. Cut wings at joint. Place in slow cooker.

2. Combine remaining ingredients. Add to slow cooker. Stir.

3. Cover. Cook on Low 5–6 hours.

Serving suggestion:

This would be great served with Aunt Mary's Baked Corn on page 133.

BBQ Chicken Sandwiches

Sarah Herr, Goshen, IN

Makes 8 servings

Prep. Time: 15 minutes ✿ *Cooking Time: 4 hours* ✿ *Ideal slow-cooker size: 5-qt.*

- 3 lb. boneless, skinless chicken thighs
- 1 onion, chopped
- ½ cup brown sugar
- ½ cup apple cider vinegar
- ½ cup ketchup
- 1 tsp. dry mustard
- 1 tsp. cumin
- 1 Tbsp. chili powder
- ½ tsp. black pepper
- 8 hamburger buns

1. Grease interior of slow-cooker crock.
2. Place chicken into crock. If you need to make a second layer, stagger the pieces so they don't directly overlap each other.
3. Mix other ingredients together well in a bowl.
4. Spoon over thighs. Make sure the ones on the bottom layer get covered too.
5. Cover. Cook on Low 4 hours, or until instant-read meat thermometer registers 160°F when stuck in center of thighs.
6. Lift cooked chicken out of crock and shred with two forks.
7. Stir shredded meat back into sauce in crock.
8. Serve on hamburger buns.

Serving suggestion:

These would be great served with Best-In-the-West Beans on page 143.

Jazzed-Up Barbecued Pulled Chicken

Hope Comerford, Clinton Township, MI

Makes 6–8 servings

Prep. Time: 5 minutes ✿ *Cooking Time: 6–7 hours* ✿ *Ideal slow-cooker size: 4-qt.*

2 lb. boneless, skinless chicken breasts
1 cup ketchup
¼ cup molasses
2 Tbsp. apple cider vinegar
2 Tbsp. Worcestershire sauce
1 clove garlic, minced
2 tsp. dry mustard
2 Tbsp. orange juice
1 tsp. orange zest

1. Place chicken in crock.

2. In a bowl, mix the ketchup, molasses, apple cider vinegar, Worcestershire sauce, minced garlic, mustard powder, orange juice, and orange zest. Pour over the chicken.

3. Cover and cook on Low for 6–7 hours.

4. Remove the chicken and shred between two forks, then stir back through the sauce in the crock.

Serving suggestions:

- Serve on buns with your favorite toppings.
- These would be great served with Macaroni Salad on page 150.

Chicken Salad Sandwiches

Rosalie Duerksen, Canton, KS

Makes 6 servings

Prep. Time: 15 minutes

12½-oz. can cooked chicken, drained
¼ cup diced celery
¼ cup golden raisins
¼ cup dried cranberries
¼ cup sliced almonds
¼ tsp. salt
⅛ tsp. pepper
¾ cup mayonnaise
6 croissants, sliced

1. In a bowl, place drained chicken. Add celery, raisins, cranberries, almonds, salt, and pepper.
2. Stir in mayonnaise until well blended.
3. Spread onto croissants.

Seafood

Grilled Barbecued Shrimp

Denise Martin, Lancaster, PA

Makes 6 servings

Prep. Time: 10 minutes · *Marinating Time: 1–2 hours* · *Grilling Time: 6 minutes*

- 1 Tbsp. Worcestershire sauce
- ½ cup olive oil
- 1 tsp. seasoning salt
- ½ tsp. Tabasco sauce
- 2 cloves garlic, minced
- 2 Tbsp. lemon juice
- 1 tsp. dried oregano
- ¼ cup ketchup
- 2 lb. large raw shrimp, peeled and deveined

1. Combine all ingredients except raw shrimp. Blend well.

2. Add shrimp to marinade. Cover and let stand 1–2 hours in the refrigerator.

3. To grill, place shrimp on a screen or grate with small holes. Grill about 3 minutes per side over medium heat, or until shrimp are bright pink, basting often.

Tip:

You can also broil the shrimp, following the directions above.

Serving suggestion:

These would be great served with Grilled Vegetables on page 136.

Crab-Topped Catfish

Vicki J. Hill, Memphis, TN

Makes 6 serving

Prep. Time: 5–10 minutes ❧ *Baking Time: 27 minutes*

6 catfish fillets (totaling 1–2 lb.)
6-oz. can white crabmeat, drained and flaked
½ cup grated Parmesan cheese
½ cup mayonnaise
1 tsp. lemon juice
Paprika
⅓ cup sliced almonds

1. Place fish on greased cookie sheet.
2. Bake, uncovered, at 350°F for 22 minutes, or until fish flakes easily with a fork. Drain.
3. Meanwhile, combine crab, cheese, mayonnaise, and lemon juice in a bowl.
4. After fish has baked for 22 minutes, spoon crab mix evenly over fish. Sprinkle with paprika and sliced almonds.
5. Return to oven and bake uncovered at 350°F for 5 minutes more.

Oven-Fried Catfish

Karen Waggoner, Joplin, MO

Makes 4 servings

Prep. Time: 15 minutes ❧ *Baking Time: 25–30 minutes*

4 catfish fillets (6 oz. each)
1 cup cornflake crumbs
¼ tsp. celery salt
½ tsp. onion powder
¼ tsp. paprika
⅛ tsp. pepper
1 egg white
2 Tbsp. milk

1. Pat fish dry with paper towels. Set aside.
2. In glass pie plate, combine crumbs, celery salt, onion powder, paprika, and pepper.
3. In a shallow bowl, beat egg white. Add milk.
4. Dip fillets in egg white mixture, then dip into crumb mixture, coating well.
5. Place in greased 9 × 13-inch baking dish.
6. Bake, uncovered, at 350°F for 25–30 minutes, or until fish flakes easily with a fork.

Serving suggestion:

This would be great served with Oven Fries on page 142.

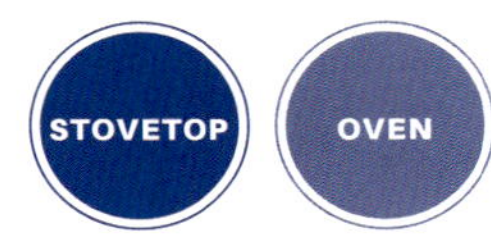

Scalloped Corn and Oysters

Evelyn Page, Lance Creek, WY

Makes 4–6 servings

Prep. Time: 5–7 minutes   *Baking Time: 60 minutes*

- 2 (15¼-oz.) cans whole kernel corn, drained
- 15¼-oz. can creamed corn
- 1 cup oysters, drained
- ¼–½ tsp. salt
- ⅛–¼ tsp. pepper
- 2-oz. jar pimentos, drained
- 8 soda crackers, crumbled
- 4 Tbsp. butter
- ¼ cup light cream, or half-and-half

1. Place a layer of half the corns followed by a layer of half the oysters in a greased 8 × 10-inch baking dish. Sprinkle with half the salt and pepper.
2. Spoon half the pimentos over top, and half the cracker crumbs.
3. Melt the butter in a small pan. Spoon half of it over the cracker crumbs.
4. Repeat the layers.
5. Pour cream over top. Drizzle with remaining butter.
6. Bake uncovered at 350°F for 1 hour.

Tex-Mex Luau

Dorothy VanDeest, Memphis, TN

Makes 6 servings

Prep. Time: 20 minutes ❧ *Cooking Time: 2–3 hours* ❧ *Ideal slow-cooker size: 3- or 4-qt.*

1½ lb. frozen firm-textured fish fillets, thawed
2 onions, thinly sliced
2 lemons, *divided*
2 Tbsp. butter, melted
2 tsp. salt
1 bay leaf
4 whole peppercorns
1 cup water

1. Cut fillets into serving portions.
2. Combine onion slices and 1 sliced lemon in butter, along with salt, bay leaf, and peppercorns. Pour into slow cooker.
3. Place fillets on top of onion and lemon slices. Add water.
4. Cover. Cook on High 2–3 hours or until fish is flaky.
5. Before serving, carefully remove fish fillets with slotted spoon. Place on heatproof plate.
6. Sprinkle with juice of half of the second lemon. Garnish with remaining lemon slices.

Serving suggestion:

This would be great served with Absolutely Creamy Spinach on page 138.

Tuna Noodle Casserole

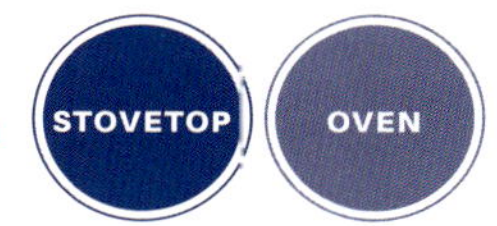

Carol Lenz, Little Chute, WI
Rosemarie Fitzgerald, Gibsonia, PA

Makes 6–8 servings

Prep. Time: 15 minutes ⁂ *Baking Time: 30–45 minutes*

2 cups dry elbow macaroni
2 (6-oz.) cans tuna, packed in water
2 (10¾-oz.) cans mushroom soup
2 cups shredded cheddar cheese
Salt to taste
Pepper to taste
1 cup frozen peas, *optional*
¾ cup cornflake crumbs, *optional*

1. Cook macaroni according to package directions. Drain. Place cooked pasta in a large mixing bowl.

2. Stir in tuna, soup, cheese, salt, pepper, and peas if you wish. Stir together gently until well mixed.

3. Place in lightly greased 2-qt. casserole. Top with cornflake crumbs if you wish.

4. Bake uncovered at 350°F for 30–45 minutes, or until heated through and bubbly.

Meatless

Baked Southwest Grits

Janie Steele, Moore, OK

Makes 8–10 servings

Prep. Time: 25 minutes ❧ *Baking Time: 45 minutes*

4 cups water
1½ tsp. salt
1 cup uncooked grits
2 eggs
4 Tbsp. (½ stick) butter
Minced garlic to taste
4-oz. can chopped green chilies
2 cups grated Mexican cheese, or Monterey Jack/cheddar combined, *divided*

1. Place water in large saucepan, add salt, and cover. Bring to boil.
2. Add grits and stir for 1 minute.
3. Cover and cook until thick and creamy, about 5–7 minutes. Stir occasionally.
4. Beat eggs in a small bowl. Stir in ¼ cup cooked grits and blend together. Add mixture to saucepan of grits.
5. Melt butter in a medium-sized pan. Stir in garlic, chilies, and 1½ cups cheese. Add to the grits mixture and stir well.
6. Spoon into a greased 2-qt. casserole. Top with remaining ½ cup cheese.
7. Bake uncovered at 350°F for 45 minutes.

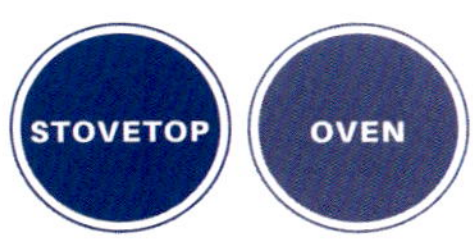

Macaroni and Cheese

Elaine Rineer, Lancaster, PA

Makes 4–6 servings

Prep. Time: 20 minutes · *Baking Time: 20–25 minutes*

- 8 oz. shell macaroni
- 3 Tbsp. butter, *divided*
- 2 Tbsp. flour
- 1 tsp. salt
- 1 tsp. dry mustard
- 2½ cups milk
- 2 cups shredded Cooper sharp, or a sharp cheddar, cheese, *divided*
- ¼ cup breadcrumbs
- Paprika

1. Cook shells according to package directions. Drain and set aside.
2. While shells are cooking, melt 2 Tbsp. butter in a large saucepan.
3. Blend in flour, salt, and dry mustard.
4. Add milk. Heat, stirring constantly until sauce thickens and is smooth.
5. Add 1½ cups cheese. Heat until melted, continuing to stir.
6. Combine sauce and cooked macaroni. Pour into a greased 2-qt. casserole.
7. Melt 1 Tbsp. butter. Stir in breadcrumbs.
8. Top macaroni and cheese with remaining cheese, buttered breadcrumbs, and paprika.
9. Bake uncovered at 375°F for 20–25 minutes.

Variation:

Use evaporated milk instead of regular milk. Use 2 Tbsp. Parmesan cheese instead of buttered breadcrumbs as topping.

—Andrea Cunningham, Arlington, KS

Creamy Mac and Cheese

Renee Hankins, Narvon, PA

Makes 6 servings

Prep. Time: 5 minutes ♣ *Cooking Time: 3–4 hours* ♣ *Ideal slow-cooker size: 5-qt.*

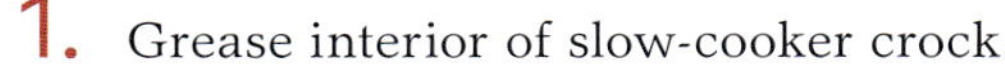

12 oz. uncooked elbow macaroni
2 cups milk
12-oz. can evaporated milk
1 small onion, chopped
½ tsp. salt
¼ tsp. black pepper
1 cup grated Gouda cheese
1½ cups grated cheddar cheese

1. Grease interior of slow-cooker crock.
2. Mix all ingredients, except Gouda and cheddar cheeses, in crock.
3. Cover. Cook on Low 3–4 hours, or until macaroni are as soft as you like them.
4. Thirty minutes before end of cooking time, stir in cheeses. Cover and continue cooking.
5. If you want a crispy top, or if water has gathered around the edges, uncover during last 30 minutes of cooking time.

Pizza Roll-Ups

Vonnie Oyer, Hubbard, OR

Makes 10 servings

Prep. Time: 30 minutes ❧ *Standing and Rising Time: 1½ hours* ❧ *Baking Time: 20–25 minutes*

1½ Tbsp. yeast
⅜ cup warm (110–115°F) water
1½ Tbsp. + ½ tsp. sugar, *divided*
1½ Tbsp. + ½ tsp. shortening
1⅓ tsp. salt
1½ cups hot (120–130°F) water
5–6 cups flour
2 cups shredded mozzarella cheese
½ tsp. salt
½ tsp. parsley
1 tsp. Italian seasoning
¼ tsp. pepper

Sauce:

2 cups tomato sauce
1½ tsp. sugar
1½ tsp. Italian seasoning
1½ tsp. parsley
1½ tsp. dried basil
½ tsp. garlic powder
¼ tsp. pepper

1. In a small bowl, dissolve yeast and ½ tsp. sugar in ⅜ cup warm water.
2. In a large bowl, combine 1½ Tbsp. sugar, shortening, salt, and hot water. Add yeast mixture.
3. Stir in flour. Knead for 10 minutes, or until smooth and elastic. Place in greased bowl, turning once.
4. Let rise to double. Punch down and let rest 10 minutes.
5. Roll dough into a 14-inch-wide strip, ¼-inch thick.
6. In a small bowl, mix cheese with ½ tsp. salt, ½ tsp. parsley, 1 tsp. Italian seasoning, and ¼ tsp. pepper. Sprinkle over dough. Press slightly into dough.
7. Roll up dough, like a jelly roll. Cut roll into 1-inch-thick slices.
8. Grease 2 baking sheets, or line with parchment paper. Place roll-ups on baking sheets, cut side up, and let stand 10–20 minutes.
9. Bake at 400°F for 20–25 minutes.
10. Mix tomato sauce and the seasonings and herbs in a saucepan. Heat. Serve roll-ups with small bowls of sauce for dunking.

Apple-Stuffed Acorn Squash

Susan Guarneri, Three Lakes, WI

Makes 4 servings

Prep. Time: 20 minutes ✿ *Baking Time: 50 minutes*

- 2 acorn squash
- 3 tart apples, *divided*
- 1 Tbsp. fresh lemon juice, taken from half a lemon (reserve the other half)
- 1½ tsp. grated lemon rind, taken from half a lemon (reserve the other half)
- 4 Tbsp. (¼ cup) melted butter, *divided*
- ⅓ cup brown sugar
- ½ tsp. salt
- 1 tsp. cinnamon

1. Cut squash in half. Scoop out seeds. Place in baking dish, cut side down, and add ½ inch boiling water. Bake, covered with aluminum foil, at 400°F for 20 minutes.
2. Pare, core, and dice 2 apples. In small bowl, mix with lemon juice, rind, 2 Tbsp. butter, and brown sugar.
3. Remove squash halves from oven. Brush cut halves with remaining 2 Tbsp. butter. Sprinkle with salt and cinnamon.
4. Fill squash halves with apple mixture.
5. Place squash halves cut side up in baking dish. Add ½ inch boiling water. Cover with foil and bake 30 minutes longer.
6. Before serving, pour pan juices over squash. Garnish each half with slices from the reserved apple and the reserved lemon half.

Soups, Stews & Chilies

Hope's Taco Soup

Hope Comerford, Clinton Township, MI

Makes 4–6 servings

Prep. Time: 20 minutes · *Cooking Time: 8 hours* · *Ideal slow-cooker size: 4-qt.*

- 1 lb. ground turkey
- 1 large onion, chopped
- Salt to taste
- Pepper to taste
- 1-oz. pkg. ranch dressing/seasoning mix
- 1 pkg. taco seasoning
- 1 tsp. cumin
- 1 tsp. garlic powder
- 1 cup pinto beans
- 15½-oz. can chili beans
- 1 cup frozen whole kernel corn
- 2 (14½-oz.) cans diced tomatoes (chili flavor)
- 4 cups beef broth or stock

1. Brown turkey meat with the onion, salt, and pepper.
2. Place the browned meat into the crock and add all the remaining ingredients. Stir.
3. Cover and cook on Low for 8 hours.

Serving suggestion:

Serve with sour cream, cheese, and tortilla chips.

Tip:

This recipe does great doubled.

Favorite Chili

Carol Eveleth, Cheyenne, WY

Makes 4–6 servings

Prep. Time: 10 minutes *Cooking Time: 35 minutes*

- 1 lb. ground beef
- 1 tsp. salt
- ½ tsp. black pepper
- 1 Tbsp. olive oil
- 1 small onion, diced
- 2 cloves garlic, minced
- 1 green pepper, chopped
- 2 Tbsp. chili powder
- ½ tsp. cumin
- 1 cup water
- 16-oz. can chili beans
- 15-oz. can crushed tomatoes

1. Press Sauté button and adjust once to Sauté More function. Wait until indicator says hot.
2. Season the ground beef with salt and black pepper.
3. Add the olive oil into the inner pot. Coat the whole bottom of the pot with the oil.
4. Add ground beef into the inner pot. The ground beef will start to release moisture. Allow the ground beef to brown and crisp slightly, stirring occasionally to break it up. Taste and adjust the seasoning with more salt and ground black pepper.
5. Add diced onion, minced garlic, chopped pepper, chili powder, and cumin. Sauté for about 5 minutes, until the spices start to release their fragrance. Stir frequently.
6. Add water and can of chili beans, not drained. Mix well. Pour in can of crushed tomatoes.
7. Close and secure lid, making sure vent is set to sealing, and pressure cook on Manual at high pressure for 10 minutes.
8. Let the pressure release naturally when cooking time is up. Open the lid carefully.

Serving suggestion:
This would be great served with Sweet Cornbread on page 167.

Split Pea Soup

Judy Gascho, Woodburn, OR

Makes 3–4 servings

Prep. Time: 20 minutes · *Cooking Time: 15 minutes* · *Recommended Instant Pot Size: 6-qt.*

4 cups chicken broth
4 sprigs thyme
4 oz. ham, diced (about ⅓ cup)
2 Tbsp. butter
2 stalks celery
2 carrots
1 large leek
3 cloves garlic
1½ cups dried green split peas (about 12 oz.)
Salt to taste
Pepper to taste

1. Pour the broth into the inner pot of the Instant Pot and set to Sauté. Add the thyme, ham, and butter.

2. While the broth heats, chop the celery and cut the carrots into ½-inch-thick rounds. Halve the leek lengthwise and thinly slice and chop the garlic. Add the vegetables to the pot as you cut them. Rinse the split peas in a colander, discarding any small stones, then add to the pot.

3. Secure the lid, making sure the steam valve is in the sealing position. Set the cooker to Manual at high pressure for 15 minutes. When the time is up, carefully turn the steam valve to the venting position to release the pressure manually.

4. Turn off the Instant Pot. Remove the lid and stir the soup; discard the thyme sprigs.

5. Thin the soup with up to one cup water if needed (the soup will continue to thicken as it cools). Season with salt and pepper.

Easy Creamy Potato and Ham Soup

Lori Klassen, Mountain Lake, MN

Makes 12 servings

Prep. Time: 15 minutes · *Cooking Time: 30 minutes*

- 6 cups water
- 7 tsp. chicken bouillon granules
- 2 (8-oz.) pkg. cream cheese, cubed
- 1½ cups cubed ham, fully cooked
- 32-oz. pkg. frozen diced hash brown potatoes
- ½ cup chopped onions
- 1 tsp. garlic powder
- 1 tsp. dill weed

1. Combine water and chicken bouillon granules in a large soup pot over heat. Stir until granules are dissolved.
2. Add cream cheese and stir until melted.
3. Add all other ingredients and simmer 20 minutes, or until vegetables are tender.

Tip:

To reduce calories, use low-fat cream cheese.

Chicken Noodle Soup

Colleen Heatwole, Burton, MI

Makes 6–8 servings

Prep. Time: 15 minutes ⁂ *Cooking Time: 4 minutes* ⁂ *Recommended Instant Pot Size: 6-qt.*

2 Tbsp. butter
1 Tbsp. oil
1 medium onion, diced
2 large carrots, diced
3 ribs celery, diced
3 cloves garlic, minced
1 tsp. thyme
1 tsp. oregano
1 tsp. basil
8 cups chicken broth
2 cups cubed cooked chicken
8 oz. medium egg noodles
1 cup frozen peas (thaw while preparing soup)
Salt to taste
Pepper to taste

1. In the inner pot of the Instant Pot, melt the butter with oil on the Sauté function.
2. Add onion, carrots, and celery with large pinch of salt and continue cooking on sauté until soft, about 5 minutes, stirring frequently.
3. Add garlic, thyme, oregano, and basil and sauté an additional minute.
4. Add broth, cooked chicken, and noodles, stirring to combine all ingredients.
5. Put lid on the Instant Pot and set vent to sealing. Select Manual high pressure and add 4 minutes.
6. When time is up do a quick (manual) release of the pressure.
7. Add thawed peas, stir, adjust seasoning with salt and pepper, and serve.

Tip:

You can also prepare chicken for this recipe in the Instant Pot, but for this recipe, I usually use leftovers.

Scrumptious White Chicken Chili

Gloria L. Lehman, Singers Glen, VA
Lauren Bailey, Mechanicsburg, PA

Makes 6 servings

Prep. Time: 20–25 minutes · *Cooking Time: 25 minutes*

1½ Tbsp. oil
1 large onion, chopped
2 cloves garlic, minced
2 cups chopped cooked chicken
4-oz. can chopped mild green chilies
½–1 Tbsp. diced jalapeño pepper, *optional*
1½ tsp. ground cumin
1 tsp. dried oregano
10½-oz. can condensed chicken broth
10½-oz. can refilled with water
15-oz. can great northern beans
½ tsp. cayenne, or to taste
Salt to taste
6 oz. shredded Monterey Jack cheese
½ cup low-fat sour cream
Chopped green onions, *optional*
Fresh cilantro, *optional*

1. In large stockpot, sauté onion and garlic in oil over medium heat.

2. Add chicken, chilies, jalapeño pepper (if you wish), cumin, oregano, chicken broth, water, and beans to stockpot and stir well. Bring to a boil, reduce heat, and simmer, covered, 10–15 minutes.

3. Just before serving, add cayenne, salt, cheese, and sour cream. Heat just until cheese is melted, being careful not to let the soup boil.

4. Serve at once, garnished with chopped green onions and fresh cilantro if desired.

Tip:

If you don't have cooked chicken, cut up 1½ lb. skinless chicken breasts (about 1½ breasts) into 1-inch chunks. Follow Step 2 and proceed with the directions as given, being sure to simmer until the chicken is no longer pink.

Three Bean Chili

Deb Kepiro, Strasburg, PA

Makes 6 servings

Prep. Time: 15 minutes ❀ *Cooking Time: 30–60 minutes*

1 large onion, chopped
2 Tbsp. oil
2 cups diced cooked chicken
15½-oz. can kidney beans, rinsed and drained
15½-oz. can pinto beans, rinsed and drained
15½-oz. can black beans, rinsed and drained
2 (14½-oz.) cans diced tomatoes
1 cup chicken broth
¾ cup salsa
1 tsp. cumin
¼ tsp. salt
Shredded cheese, *optional*
Green onions, *optional*
Sour cream, *optional*

1. In a soup pot, sauté onion in oil until tender.
2. Add chicken, beans, tomatoes, broth, salsa, cumin, and salt.
3. Bring to a boil. Cover. Reduce heat and let simmer for 30–60 minutes.
4. If desired, garnish with shredded cheese, green onions, and sour cream.

Variation:

Add 1 cup corn, 1 Tbsp. chili powder, and 15½-oz. can undrained chili beans. Use 1 lb. ground beef, browned, instead of chicken.

—Moreen Weaver, Bath, NY

Manhattan Clam Chowder

Joyce Slaymaker, Strasburg, PA
Louise Stackhouse, Benton, PA

Makes 8 servings

Prep. Time: 15 minutes ❧ *Cooking Time: 8–10 hours* ❧ *Ideal slow-cooker size: 3½-qt.*

¼ lb. salt pork, or bacon, diced and fried
1 large onion, chopped
2 carrots, thinly sliced
3 ribs celery, sliced
1 Tbsp. dried parsley flakes
28-oz. can tomatoes
½ tsp. salt
2–3 (8-oz.) cans clams with liquid
2 whole peppercorns
1 bay leaf
1½ tsp. dried crushed thyme
3 medium potatoes, cubed

1. Combine all ingredients in slow cooker.

2. Cover. Cook on Low 8–10 hours. Remove bay leaf before serving.

Creamed Crab and Corn Soup

Shari Jensen, Fountain, CO

Makes 8 servings

Prep. Time: 15 minutes ❧ *Cooking Time: 25–30 minutes*

- 1 lb. lump crabmeat
- 4 Tbsp. (¼ cup) butter
- 1½ cups finely chopped onions
- 2 Tbsp. flour
- 8 cups corn (freshly cut from cob is best*)
- 4 cups heavy cream
- 2 cups chicken broth
- ¼ tsp. thyme
- Salt to taste
- White pepper to taste
- 2 Tbsp. chopped parsley
- Grated cheddar cheese

1. Pick over crabmeat to remove any shell or cartilage. Set aside.
2. In large stockpot, melt butter. Add onions and sauté until clear and tender.
3. Blend in flour. Add corn kernels. Cook for 5 minutes, stirring frequently.
4. Add cream, broth, thyme, salt, and pepper. Cook over medium heat for 10 minutes, or until corn is tender. Stir often to prevent broth from scorching.
5. Add crabmeat and parsley and cook until meat is thoroughly heated.
6. Serve hot. Garnish with cheddar cheese.

Tips:

- One good-sized ear of sweet corn will yield 1–1½ cups corn kernels.
- Don't use high heat or cream will scald.

Salmon Chowder

Millie Martin, Mount Joy, PA
Betty K. Drescher, Quakertown, PA

Makes 6 servings

Prep. Time: 15–20 minutes ❧ *Cooking Time: 35 minutes*

- 3 potatoes, diced
- 2 Tbsp. minced onion
- 2 Tbsp. diced celery
- 1 lb. can salmon, no salt added
- ½ cup corn
- 1 tsp. sage
- 1 tsp. dried basil
- Pepper to taste
- 1 qt. skim milk
- 2 Tbsp. chopped fresh parsley
- Lemon zest, *optional*

1. In stockpot, cook potatoes, onions, and celery in small amount of water until tender.
2. Empty salmon into bowl. Remove bones and skin from salmon. Pull fish apart into pieces.
3. Add salmon, corn, sage, basil, pepper, and milk to vegetables in stockpot.
4. Cover. Heat slowly until very hot.
5. Top with chopped parsley, and lemon zest if you wish.

Oyster Stew

Dorothy Reise, Severna Park, MD

Makes 4 servings

Prep. Time: 10–15 minutes ⁂ *Cooking Time: 15 minutes*

- 2–3 doz. fresh oysters in liquid
- 2 Tbsp. butter
- 1 Tbsp. chopped onion
- 3 Tbsp. flour
- 3 cups milk
- 1 tsp. salt
- ½ tsp. pepper
- ½ tsp. chopped parsley
- Pinch celery seed, *optional*
- Dash paprika, *optional*

1. In a small skillet over medium heat, pre-cook oysters in their own liquid until edges curl and oysters become plump. Set aside.

2. In large stockpot, melt butter. Add onion and sauté until soft.

3. Over medium heat, add flour and stir until smooth.

4. Slowly add milk, stirring constantly until thickened.

5. Add the pre-cooked oysters and liquid, salt, pepper, parsley, and celery seed and paprika if you wish. Mix well.

6. Heat thoroughly and serve.

Harvest Corn Chowder

Flossie Sultzaberger, Mechanicsburg, PA

Makes 10 servings

Prep. Time: 20 minutes ❧ *Cooking Time: 40 minutes*

1 medium onion, chopped

1 Tbsp. trans-fat–free tub margarine

2 (14½-oz.) cans no-salt-added cream-style corn

4 cups no-salt-added whole kernel corn

4 cups peeled, diced potatoes

6-oz. jar sliced mushrooms, drained

½ medium green pepper, chopped

½–1 medium sweet red pepper, chopped

10¾-oz. can lower-sodium, lower-fat mushroom soup

3 cups fat-free milk

Pepper to taste

½ lb. bacon, cooked and crumbled

1. In a large saucepan, sauté onion in margarine until tender.
2. Add cream-style corn, kernel corn, potatoes, mushrooms, peppers, soup, and milk. Add pepper, to taste.
3. Simmer 30 minutes or until vegetables are tender.
4. To serve, garnish with bacon.

Corn Chowder

Janie Steele, Moore, OK

Makes 7 servings

Prep. Time: 30–35 minutes · *Cooking Time: 5¼–6½ hours* · *Ideal slow-cooker size: 3½- or 4-qt.*

- 4 large ears of corn, corn cut off cob, or 1-lb. bag frozen whole-kernel corn, thawed
- 1 large onion, chopped
- 1 celery rib, chopped
- 1 Tbsp. butter
- 1½ cups cubed potatoes
- 1 cup water
- 2 tsp. chicken bouillon granules
- ½ tsp. salt
- ¼ tsp. dried thyme
- ¼ tsp. pepper
- 6 Tbsp. flour
- 3 cups milk

1. Combine all ingredients in slow cooker except flour and milk.

2. Cook on Low 5–6 hours, or until potatoes are tender.

3. Mix flour and milk until smooth. Stir into corn chowder slowly until thickened. Cook 15–30 minutes more.

Creamy Potato Soup

Hope Comerford, Clinton Township, MI

Makes 6 servings

Prep. Time: 20 minutes · *Cooking Time: 8–10 hours* · *Ideal slow-cooker size: 5-qt.*

- 8–9 Idaho potatoes, chopped into bite-sized pieces
- 4½ cups low-sodium chicken broth or stock
- ½ cup low-fat milk
- 1 medium onion, chopped
- 2–4 carrots, chopped
- 1–2 stalks celery, chopped
- 3 green onions, chopped
- 8-oz. block reduced-fat cream cheese, chopped into cubes
- ¼ cup nonfat plain Greek yogurt
- 3 Tbsp. cornstarch
- 2 Tbsp. butter
- 2 tsp. garlic powder
- 1 tsp. onion powder
- 1½ tsp. pepper
- 1 tsp. salt

1. Place all ingredients into your crock and stir.
2. Cook on Low for 8–10 hours.

Serving suggestion:

Serve with fresh chopped chives or green onions on top and little bit of shredded cheese.

Tip:

Use an immersion blender to give your soup a smoother and creamier texture.

Broccoli Cheese Soup

Hope Comerford, Clinton Township, MI

Makes 6 servings

Prep. Time: 15 minutes ❧ *Cooking Time: 6–7 hours* ❧ *Ideal slow-cooker size: 3-qt.*

- 1 head broccoli, chopped into tiny pieces
- 1 onion, chopped finely
- 2 (12-oz.) cans evaporated milk
- 10¾-oz. can condensed cheddar cheese soup
- 3 cups water
- 4 chicken bouillon cubes
- 1½ tsp. garlic powder
- 1 tsp. onion powder
- ½ tsp. seasoned salt
- 1 tsp. pepper
- 16-oz. block Velveeta cheese, chopped into pieces

1. Place all ingredients into crock, except for the Velveeta cheese, and stir.

2. Cover and cook on Low for 6–7 hours.

3. About 5–10 minutes before eating, turn slow cooker to High and stir in Velveeta cheese until melted.

Vegetables

Aunt Mary's Baked Corn

Becky Frey, Lebanon, PA
Doris Beachy, Stevens, PA
Cynthia Morris, Grottoes, VA
Susie Nisley, Millersburg, OH

Makes 4–5 servings
Makes 1½–2-qt. casserole

Prep. Time: 15 minutes ❧ *Standing Time: 1 hour* ❧ *Baking Time: 1 hour*

- 1½ cups milk
- 3 Tbsp. butter
- 3 cups creamed corn, fresh, frozen, or canned
- 3 Tbsp. cornstarch
- 3 eggs, beaten
- 2 Tbsp. sugar
- 1 tsp. salt
- ⅛ tsp. pepper

1. In a small saucepan, heat milk until it forms a skin but does not boil. Stir in butter.

2. While butter melts, mix corn and cornstarch in a good-sized mixing bowl until cornstarch is dissolved. Add beaten eggs, sugar, and seasonings. Mix in milk and butter.

3. Put in a greased 1½–2-qt. baking dish.

4. Let stand for 1 hour.

5. Bake, uncovered, at 350°F for 1 hour, or until set in the middle.

Serving suggestions:

This would be great served alongside Barbecued Pork Ribs on page 59 and Heavenly Barbecued Chicken Wings on page 84.

Slow-Cooker Corn on the Cob

Donna Conto, Saylorsburg, PA

Makes 3–4 servings

Prep. Time: 10 minutes ❧ *Cooking Time: 2–3 hours* ❧ *Ideal slow-cooker size: 5- or 6-qt.*

6–8 ears of corn (in husk)
½ cup water

1. Remove silk from corn, as much as possible, but leave husks on.
2. Cut off ends of corn and stand the ears upright in the cooker.
3. Add water to crock.
4. Cover. Cook on Low 2–3 hours.

Serving suggestions:

This would be great served alongside Taco Meatloaf on page 43 and Barbecued Chicken on page 76.

Marge's Cauliflower

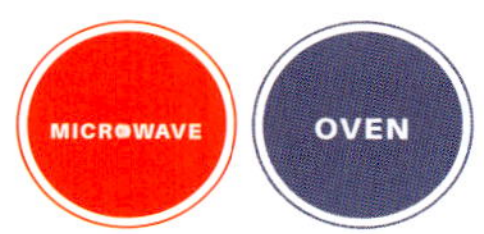

Pat Taylor, Paw Paw, WV

Makes 4 servings

Prep. Time: 30 minutes · *Cooking/Baking Time: 25 minutes*

1 fresh head of cauliflower
Water
½ cup butter, melted
1 cup dry breadcrumbs
1 tsp. Italian seasoning
1 cup shredded cheddar cheese

1. Separate cauliflower into florets. Place in microwavable dish. Sprinkle with 1 Tbsp. water. Cover and cook on high for 3–4 minutes

2. Drain florets and allow to cool until you can handle them.

3. Place melted butter in a shallow dish. Mix the breadcrumbs and seasoning together in another shallow dish.

4. Dip each floret into melted butter, and then into the seasoned breadcrumbs, rolling to cover well.

5. Place in greased 9 × 13-inch baking dish. Bake, uncovered, at 375°F for 20 minutes. Turn off oven. Sprinkle with shredded cheese and return to oven to melt.

Serving suggestion:

This would be great served alongside Baked Pork Chops with Gravy (page 65).

Grilled Vegetables

Deborah Heatwole, Waynesboro, GA

Makes 4 servings

Prep. Time: about 15–30 minutes ❧ *Grilling Time: 15–25 minutes*

- 4 cups sliced fresh summer squash and/or zucchini
- 4 cups sliced sweet onions, such as Vidalia
- 3–4 Tbsp. olive, or canola, oil
- 1–2 Tbsp. red wine vinegar
- Salt to taste
- Pepper to taste

1. Toss all ingredients in a large bowl until vegetables are evenly coated with oil and vinegar. Season with salt and pepper to taste.

2. Spray a grill basket with nonstick cooking spray. Place on grill rack over hot coals.

3. Pour vegetables into basket, replace grill lid, and cook 15–25 minutes, until vegetables reach desired doneness, stirring every 4–5 minutes.

Serving suggestions:

These would be great served alongside Grilled Burgers on page 48 and Grilled Barbecued Shrimp on page 93.

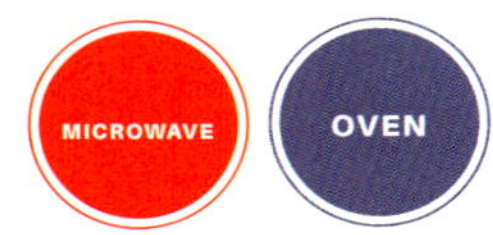

Absolutely Creamy Spinach

Vicki J. Hill, Memphis, TN

Makes 9 servings

Prep. Time: 5 minutes ❧ *Cooking/Baking Time: 8–30 minutes*

4 (10-oz.) pkg. frozen chopped spinach, thawed and squeezed dry

8-oz. pkg. cream cheese

1 stick (8 Tbsp.) butter

Fine breadcrumbs

Sprinkle paprika, *optional*

1. Place spinach in lightly greased 2-qt. baking dish.

2. Soften cream cheese and butter in microwave for 1 minute. Beat until combined. Pour over spinach.

3. Sprinkle with crumbs, and paprika if desired.

4. Heat uncovered in oven at 350°F for 20–30 minutes, or in the microwave, covered, for 8–10 minutes.

Serving suggestions:
This would be great served alongside Finger-Lickin' Spareribs on page 60 and Tex-Mex Luau on page 98.

Collard Greens with Bacon

Hope Comerford, Clinton Township, MI

Makes 8–10 servings

Prep. Time: 15 minutes · *Cooking Time: 5–6 hours* · *Ideal slow-cooker size: 3-qt.*

- 3 lb. collard greens, tough stems cut away and washed thoroughly
- 8 oz. bacon, cooked, chopped
- 1½ cups chopped onion
- 4–5 cloves garlic, chopped
- 1 cup chicken stock
- 1 cup chopped tomatoes
- 3 Tbsp. apple cider vinegar
- 2 tsp. sea salt
- ¼ tsp. pepper
- 1 tsp. sugar
- 1 bay leaf

1. Tear the collard greens into large pieces and place in the crock.

2. Place all the remaining ingredients in the crock and stir.

3. Cover and cook on Low for 5–6 hours.

Serving suggestion:

These would be great served alongside Pulled Pork on page 61.

Barbecued Green Beans

Sharon Timpe, Jackson, WI
Ruth E. Martin, Loysville, PA

Makes 10–12 servings

Prep. Time: 15 minutes ⁂ *Cooking Time: 3–4 hours* ⁂ *Ideal slow-cooker size: 4-qt.*

- 3 (14½-oz.) cans cut green beans (drain 2 cans completely; reserve liquid from 1 can)
- 1 small onion, diced
- 1 cup ketchup
- ¾ cup brown sugar
- 4 strips bacon, cooked crisp and crumbled

1. Combine green beans, diced onion, ketchup, and brown sugar in your slow cooker.
2. Add ⅓ cup of reserved bean liquid. Mix gently.
3. Cover and cook on Low 3–4 hours until beans are heated through. Stir at the end of 2 hours of cooking, if you're home.
4. Pour in a little reserved bean juice if the sauce thickens more than you like.
5. Sprinkle bacon over beans just before serving.

Serving suggestions:

These would be great served alongside So-Good Sloppy Joes on page 47 and Chicken Monterey on page 83.

Tip:

Use 1½ lb. fresh green beans instead of canned beans. When using fresh beans, you'll need to increase the cooking time to 5–6 hours on Low depending upon how soft or crunchy you like your beans.

Oven Fries

Sherry H. Kauffman, Minot, ND

Makes 6 servings

Prep. Time: 15 minutes ❧ *Baking Time: 25 minutes*

3 medium unpeeled baking potatoes (1½ lb.)

2 large carrots, peeled

2 tsp. vegetable, or canola, oil

¼ tsp. salt

¼ tsp. pepper

1. Scrub potatoes. Cut potatoes and carrots into 3½ × ½-inch strips. Pat dry with paper towel.

2. Combine oil, salt, and pepper in large bowl. Add potatoes and carrots. Toss to coat.

3. Arrange in a single layer on a baking sheet coated with nonfat cooking spray.

4. Bake at 475°F for 25 minutes, or until tender and brown, turning after 15 minutes.

Serving suggestions:

These would be great served alongside Hoosier Lamb Chops on page 37 and Oven-Fried Catfish on page 95.

Best-in-the-West Beans

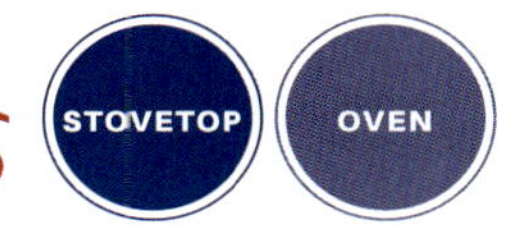

Lorraine Martin, Dryden, MI

Makes 10 servings, about 2/3 cup per serving

Prep. Time: 20 minutes ஃ *Baking Time: 1 hour*

- ½ lb. ground beef
- 5 slices bacon, chopped
- ½ cup chopped onion
- ¼ cup brown sugar
- ¼ cup white sugar
- ¼ cup no-salt ketchup
- ¼ cup barbecue sauce
- 2 Tbsp. mustard
- 2 Tbsp. molasses
- ½ tsp. chili powder
- ½ tsp. pepper
- 1-lb. can kidney beans
- 1-lb. can butter beans
- 1-lb. can pork and beans

1. Brown ground beef and bacon. Drain. Add onion and cook until tender. Add all other ingredients except beans and mix well.

2. Drain kidney beans and butter beans. Add all beans to meat mixture. Pour into 3-qt. casserole dish.

3. Bake at 350°F for 1 hour.

Tip:

To prepare in slow cooker, cook on High for 1 hour. Reduce heat to Low and cook for 4 hours.

Serving suggestions:

These would be great served alongside Deep, Dark & Delicious Barbecue Sandwiches on page 40 and BBQ Chicken Sandwiches on page 86.

American Beans

Jane Geigley, Lancaster, PA

Makes 4–6 servings

Prep. Time: 30 minutes ❀ *Cooking Time: 2 hours* ❀ *Ideal slow-cooker size: 3-qt.*

1 lb. ground beef, browned
16-oz. can pork and beans
16-oz. can kidney beans
1 qt. tomato juice
1 pt. corn
½ cup brown sugar
2 Tbsp. mustard
Chili powder to taste
1 tsp. salt
1 tsp. pepper

1. Pour each ingredient into slow cooker.
2. Stir and cook on High for 2 hours.

Serving suggestions:

- Serve over baked potatoes or cornbread.
- These would also be great served alongside Smoked Barbecue Pork Sandwiches on page 62.

Slow-Cooked Baked Beans

Hope Comerford, Clinton Township, MI

Makes 15–20 servings

Soaking time: 12 hours · *Prep. Time: 10 minutes*
Cooking Time: 12 or more hours · *Ideal slow-cooker size: 6-qt.*

2 lb. navy beans
12 oz. salt pork, chopped into small strips, *divided*
1 large onion, chopped, *divided*
¾ cup dark brown sugar
1 cup ketchup
3 Tbsp. mustard
7 cups water

1. Sort the beans to make sure there are no rocks or bad beans.
2. Soak the beans in water for 12 or more hours, with enough water to cover them plus four inches.
3. Spray crock with nonstick spray.
4. Place half of the salt pork at the bottom, then half the beans, then half the onion.
5. In a bowl, mix the brown sugar, ketchup, and mustard. Pour half of this over the contents of the crock.
6. Place the rest of the salt pork into the crock, then the remaining beans, onions, and sauce.
7. Pour in the 7 cups of water.
8. Cover and cook on Low for 12 or more hours. You will know these are done when your mixture has turned nice and brown and has thickened.

Serving suggestions:

These would be great served alongside Smoky Brisket on page 38 and Oven Barbecued Chicken on page 75.

Tip:

If you can't find salt pork, use thick-cut bacon instead.

Salads & Slaws

Strawberry Gelatin Salad

Vonda Ebersole, Mt. Pleasant Mills, PA

Makes 12 servings

Prep. Time: 15 minutes ❧ *Chilling Time: 3–4 hours*

2 cups water
6-oz. box strawberry gelatin
4 cups fresh or frozen strawberries
15-oz. can crushed pineapple, undrained
3 large bananas, sliced

1. Bring water to a boil in a saucepan Stir gelatin into boiling water until dissolved.

2. Stir in additional ingredients. Pour into a 9 × 13-inch baking pan.

3. Refrigerate until gelatin is firm.

Tip:

If you're in a hurry, use frozen strawberries. They'll speed up the gelling process.

Macaroni Salad

Frances & Cathy Kruba, Dundalk, MD
Marcia S. Myer, Manheim, PA

Makes 8–10 servings

Prep. Time: 30 minutes ⁂ *Cooking Time for pasta: 15 minutes*

1 lb. macaroni, cooked and cooled
1 cup diced celery
1 cup diced onions
1 cup diced carrots
12 hard-boiled eggs, diced
2 cups sugar
½ cup vinegar, or lemon juice
2 cups mayonnaise

Dressing:
5 eggs
1 Tbsp. mustard
1 Tbsp. butter
½–1 tsp. salt

1. Mix together macaroni, celery, onions, carrots, hard-boiled eggs, sugar, and vinegar or lemon juice. Add mayonnaise.

2. In a saucepan, mix eggs, mustard, butter, and salt. Cook on medium heat until thickened and steaming, stirring constantly. Do not boil.

3. Remove from heat and cool 5 minutes. Add to macaroni mixture.

Tips:

- Grate the carrots instead of dicing them.
- Reduce the sugar by a half-cup if desired.

Serving suggestions:

This would be great served alongside Deep, Dark & Delicious Barbecue Sandwiches on page 40 and Jazzed-Up Barbecue Pulled Chicken on page 87.

Creamy Dill Pasta Salad

Jan Mast, Lancaster, PA

Makes 10 servings

Prep. Time: 15 minutes ❧ *Cooking Time: 12–15 minutes*

3 cups uncooked tri-color spiral pasta
6-oz. can black olives, halved and drained
½ cup chopped red pepper
½ cup chopped green pepper
½ cup chopped onions
2 tomatoes, chopped
1 Tbsp. dill weed

Dressing:

¾ cup mayonnaise
2 Tbsp. prepared mustard
¼ cup vinegar
⅓ cup sugar

1. Cook pasta according to package directions, being careful not to overcook. Rinse in cool water. Drain well. Place in large mixing bowl.
2. Add vegetables and dill weed and toss.
3. In a mixing bowl, combine mayonnaise, mustard, vinegar, and sugar.
4. Pour over pasta and vegetables and stir to coat.
5. Chill and serve.

Serving suggestions:

This would be great served alongside Grilled Burgers on page 48 and Crispy Chicken on page 73.

Summer Pasta Salad

Judy Govotsos, Frederick, MD

Makes 15–18 servings

Prep. Time: 8–10 minutes · *Cooking Time: 15 minutes*

- 1 lb. uncooked penne or corkscrew pasta
- 1 yellow pepper, sliced
- 1 green pepper, sliced
- 1 red pepper, sliced
- 1 red onion, sliced
- 8 oz. crumbled feta cheese, *optional*
- ½ lb. pitted Kalamata olives, *optional*
- Cherry tomatoes, *optional*
- 16-oz. bottle Caesar salad dressing
- 10-oz. pkg. chicken strips, cooked, *optional*

1. Cook pasta according to package directions. Drain.
2. In a large mixing bowl, combine all ingredients except salad dressing and chicken.
3. Pour dressing over pasta mixture. Toss.
4. Add chicken immediately before serving.

Variations:

- Instead of yellow and red peppers, substitute 2 cups cut-up broccoli florets in Step 2.
- Instead of feta cheese, use 1 cup shredded cheddar cheese.
- Instead of Caesar salad dressing, use three-cheese ranch dressing.

—Lois Smith, Millersville, PA

Pasta Salad with Tuna

Sheila Soldner, Lititz, PA

Makes 6–8 servings

Prep. Time: 15 minutes · *Cooking Time: 15 minutes*

- ½ lb. uncooked rotini pasta
- 12½-oz. can solid white tuna, drained and flaked
- 2 cups thinly sliced cucumber
- 1 large tomato, seeded and sliced, or ½ pint cherry or grape tomatoes
- ½ cup sliced celery
- ¼ cup chopped green pepper
- ¼ cup sliced green onions
- 1 cup bottled Italian dressing
- ¼ cup mayonnaise
- 1 Tbsp. prepared mustard
- 1 tsp. dill weed
- 1 tsp. salt
- ⅛ tsp. pepper

1. Prepare rotini according to package directions. Drain.

2. In a large bowl, combine rotini, tuna, cucumbers, tomato, celery, green pepper, and onions.

3. In a small bowl, blend together Italian dressing, mayonnaise, mustard, and seasonings. Add to salad mixture. Toss to coat.

4. Cover and chill. Toss gently before serving.

Spring Pea Salad

Dottie Schmidt, Kansas City, MO

Makes 4 servings

Prep. Time: 20 minutes ⁂ *Chilling Time: 30 minutes*

- 10-oz. pkg. frozen peas
- 1 cup diced celery
- 1 cup chopped fresh cauliflower florets
- ¼ cup diced green onions
- 1 cup chopped cashews
- ¼ cup crisp-cooked and crumbled bacon
- ¼ cup sour cream

Dressing:

- ½ cup ranch salad dressing
- ¼ tsp. Dijon mustard
- 1 small clove garlic, minced

1. Thaw peas. Drain.
2. In a large mixing bowl, combine peas, celery, cauliflower, onion, cashews, and bacon with sour cream.
3. In a small bowl, mix the ranch dressing, mustard, and minced garlic. Begin by pouring only half the dressing over salad mixture. Toss gently. Add more if needed. (The dressing amount is generous.) Chill before serving.

Serving suggestions:

This would be great served alongside Ham Loaf on page 69 and Baked Chicken Fingers on page 74.

Potato Salad

Gladys Shank, Harrisonburg, VA
Sheila Soldner, Lititz, PA
Sue Suter, Millersville, PA

Makes 8–10 servings

Prep. Time: 20–30 minutes · *Cooking Time: 45 minutes* · *Cooling Time: 3–4 hours*

8 medium-sized potatoes, diced, peeled or unpeeled
1½ tsp. salt
4 hard-boiled eggs, diced
½–1 cup chopped celery
¼–1 cup chopped onions

Dressing:
2 eggs, beaten
¾ cup sugar
1 tsp. cornstarch
⅓ cup vinegar
⅓ cup milk
3 Tbsp. butter
1 tsp. prepared mustard
1 cup mayonnaise

1. Cooked diced potatoes in salt water to a firm softness (don't let them get mushy). Cool.
2. Peel and dice hard-boiled eggs.
3. Mix cooled potatoes and eggs with celery and onions.
4. Mix eggs, sugar, cornstarch, vinegar, and milk in a saucepan and cook until thickened. Add butter, mustard, and mayonnaise. Cool.
5. Pour cooled dressing over potatoes, eggs, celery, and onions.
6. Refrigerate and chill for several hours before serving.

Serving suggestion:

This would be great served alongside Barbecued Chicken on page 76.

Variations:

- Stir 1 tsp. celery seed into the dressing (Step 4), or substitute celery seed for the celery if you wish.
  —Ruth Schrock, Shipshewana, IN
- Shred the potatoes after they're cooked instead of cubing them before they're cooked. And substitute 1/3 cup sour cream for the milk in the dressing.
  —Martha Belle Burkholder, Waynesboro, VA

Easy Red Potato Salad

Becky Harder, Monument, CO

Makes 6 servings

Prep. Time: 20 minutes ⁂ *Cooking Time: 20 minutes* ⁂ *Standing Time: 30 minutes*

2 lb. red potatoes
⅓ cup cider vinegar
2 medium-sized ribs of celery, chopped
1/3 cup sliced green onions, including some green tops
½ cup mayonnaise
½ cup sour cream
1½ tsp. salt
½ tsp. pepper
Sprinkle paprika

1. Place potatoes in pot and cover with water. Cover and bring to a boil over high heat. Reduce heat to medium-low. Cover and simmer 10 minutes, or until potatoes are tender in the center. Drain and cool.
2. Cut potatoes into quarters, or eighths if they're large. Place in large mixing bowl. Pour vinegar over them and stir.
3. Let the potatoes stand for 30 minutes while you prepare the celery and onions. Stir the potatoes occasionally.
4. Mix mayonnaise, sour cream, salt, and pepper together in a small bowl.
5. Add the celery and onions to the potatoes. Toss gently.
6. Stir in dressing and mix gently. Sprinkle with a dash of paprika. Chill until ready to serve.

Serving suggestion:

This would be great served alongside Smoky Brisket on page 38.

Variations:

- Add 3 hard-boiled eggs, chopped, to Step 5.
- Use ¾ tsp. celery seed instead of the chopped celery.

—Lori Newswanger, Lancaster, PA

Creamy Coleslaw

Tammy Yoder, Belleville, PA

Makes 6 servings

Prep. Time: 10 minutes ❧ *Chilling Time: 30 minutes*

½ head cabbage
½ cup mayonnaise
2 Tbsp. vinegar
⅓ cup sugar
Pinch salt
Pinch pepper
1 Tbsp. celery seed, or to taste
¼ cup grated carrots

1. Shred cabbage. Place in a large mixing bowl.
2. Mix all remaining ingredients together in another bowl.
3. Stir dressing into shredded cabbage, mixing well.
4. Chill for 30 minutes before serving.

Variations:

- If you're short on time, use a bag of prepared shredded cabbage with carrots.
- For added zest, stir ½ tsp. dry mustard into the dressing in Step 2.

—Maricarol Magill, Freehold, NJ

Broccoli Slaw

Bonnie Heatwole, Springs, PA

Makes 8 servings

Prep. Time: 15 minutes

16-oz. pkg. broccoli slaw
1 cup sunflower seeds
1 cup slivered almonds
2 (3-oz.) pkg. chicken-flavored Ramen noodles
1 cup diced green onions

Dressing:

½ cup oil
⅓ cup white vinegar
½ cup sugar
2 seasoning packets from Ramen noodles

1. Combine salad ingredients in a large bowl.

2. Shake the dressing ingredients together in a jar with a tight-fitting lid. (The dressing is probably more than needed for the amount of salad, so begin by adding only half of what you've made. Add more if you need it.) Add the dressing right before serving. Toss to mix.

Serving suggestion:

This would be great served alongside Reuben Casserole on page 51.

Breads

Monkey Bread

Sheila Heil, Lancaster, PA

Makes 12 servings

Prep. Time: 20 minutes · *Baking Time: 30 minutes* · *Cooling Time: 10 minutes*

- ½ cup sugar
- 1 tsp. cinnamon
- 3 (7½-oz.) cans refrigerated buttermilk biscuits
- 1 cup brown sugar
- ¾ cup melted butter or margarine

1. Heat oven to 350°F. Lightly grease a 12-cup fluted tube, or Bundt, pan.
2. Mix sugar and cinnamon together in plastic bag.
3. Separate dough into 30 biscuits. Cut each into quarters.
4. Shake 3 or 4 biscuit pieces at a time in the bag to coat.
5. Arrange coated pieces in pan.
6. In a small mixing bowl, mix brown sugar and butter together and pour over biscuit pieces.
7. Bake 28–32 minutes, or until golden brown and no longer doughy in center.
8. Cool in pan for 10 minutes.
9. Turn upside down onto a serving plate. Serve warm, allowing each person at the table to pull off pieces to eat.

Banana Bread

Margaret Moffitt, Bartlett, TN

Makes 1 loaf, or about 10 slices

Prep. Time: 30 minutes  *Baking Time: 30 minutes*

- 1½ sticks (¾ cup) butter, softened
- 1 cup sugar
- 3 bananas, mashed
- 1 cup jam (blackberry works well)
- 2 eggs, well beaten
- 2 cups flour
- 1 tsp. baking soda
- ¾ cup chopped pecans

1. In a large mixing bowl, cream butter and sugar together. Add mashed bananas, jam, and eggs, and blend well.

2. In a separate bowl, sift flour and baking soda together. Add to wet ingredients. When well mixed, stir in nuts.

3. Line the bottom of a 9 × 5-inch loaf pan with waxed paper.

4. Bake at 350°F for approximately 30 minutes, or until tester inserted in center of top of loaf comes out clean.

5. Allow to cool in pan for 10 minutes. Then remove loaf and continue cooling on wire rack.

Sweet Cornbread

Hope Comerford, Clinton Township, MI

Makes 6 servings

Prep. Time: 10 minutes ⁂ *Cooking Time: 3½–4 hours* ⁂ *Ideal slow-cooker size: 3-qt.*

- 1 cup cornmeal
- 1 cup flour
- ⅔ cup sugar
- 2 tsp. baking powder
- 3 Tbsp. butter, melted
- ¼ cup vegetable oil
- 1 egg
- 1–2 Tbsp. honey
- 1 cup milk
- ¼ cup frozen corn, *optional*

1. In a bowl, mix the cornmeal, flour, sugar, and baking powder.
2. Next, add the melted butter, vegetable oil, egg, honey, and milk and mix it up.
3. Add the corn (if using) and stir again.
4. Grease your crock with nonstick spray and pour in the batter.
5. Cover and cook on Low for 3½–4 hours.

Serving suggestion:

This would be great served alongside Favorite Chili on page 112.

Sour Cream Cornbread

Ida H. Goering, Dayton, VA

Makes 12 servings

Prep. Time: 10–15 minutes *Baking Time: 20–22 minutes*

¾ cup yellow cornmeal
1 cup flour
1 tsp. baking soda
1 tsp. cream of tartar
1 tsp. salt
3 Tbsp. sugar
1 egg, well beaten
1 cup sour cream
½ cup milk
3 Tbsp. butter, melted

1. Preheat oven to 400°F.
2. Grease a 9 × 9-inch, or 7 × 11-inch, baking pan.
3. Measure cornmeal into a mixing bowl and sift into it the flour, baking soda, cream of tartar, salt, and sugar.
4. In a separate bowl, beat egg well, and then add sour cream, milk, and melted butter.
5. Pour wet ingredients into flour mixture. Stir just until well mixed.
6. Pour into baking pan.
7. Bake at 400°F for 20–22 minutes, or until tester inserted in center of bread comes out clean.
8. Serve hot.

Serving suggestion:
This would be great served alongside Texas Cottage Pie on page 53.

Tips:

- Leftovers can be split into pieces, buttered lightly, and placed under the broiler until browned. Delicious!
- For breakfast, serve the cornbread with sausage gravy and fried apples on the side. For a main meal, serve it with smoked sausage, steamed cabbage, pinto beans, and applesauce.

Buttery Soft Pretzels

Mary Sommerfeld, Lancaster, PA

Makes 12 pretzels

Prep. Time: 20 minutes ⁂ *Standing and Rising Time: 70 minutes* ⁂ *Baking Time: 8 minutes*

4 tsp. dry yeast
1 tsp. + ½ cup, sugar, *divided*
1¼ cups warm (110°F) water
5 cups flour
1½ tsp. salt
1 Tbsp. vegetable oil
½ cup baking soda
4 cups hot water
Salt to taste
2 tsp. butter, melted

1. Dissolve yeast and 1 tsp. sugar in warm water. Let stand 10 minutes.

2. In large mixing bowl, mix flour, ½ cup sugar, and salt. Make a well in the center.

3. Add yeast mixture and oil to dry ingredients. Mix well. If dry, add several tablespoons water.

4. Knead dough 7–8 minutes, until elastic. Place in oiled bowl and cover. Let rise in a warm, draft-free place until double, about 1 hour.

5. Preheat oven to 450°F.

6. Dissolve baking soda in hot water in large bowl.

7. Divide dough into 12 pieces. Roll each into a long, thin rope—about 20-inch long—on an un-floured surface. Shape each into a pretzel.

8. Dip in soda-water solution and place on greased baking sheet. Sprinkle with salt.

9. Bake 8 minutes until browned. Brush with melted butter.

Desserts

Chocolate Chip Cookies

Mary Martins, Fairbank, IA

Makes 3 dozen big cookies

Prep. Time: 15 minutes ✿ *Baking Time: 9 minutes per sheet* ✿ *Chilling Time: 1 hour*

- 2 sticks (1 cup) butter, at room temperature
- 1 cup brown sugar
- 1 cup sugar
- 3 eggs, beaten
- 3½ cups flour
- 2 tsp. cream of tartar
- 2 tsp. baking soda
- ½ tsp. salt
- 1 tsp. vanilla extract
- 12-oz. pkg. chocolate chips
- 1 cup chopped nuts, *optional*

1. In a large mixing bowl, combine butter, sugars, and eggs.
2. In a separate mixing bowl, sift together flour, cream of tartar, baking soda, and salt.
3. Add about one-third of the dry ingredients to the creamed mixture. Mix well. Add half of the remaining dry ingredients and mix well. Add the remaining dry ingredients and mix until thoroughly blended.
4. Stir in vanilla, chocolate chips, and nuts (if using). Chill in the fridge for 60 minutes.
5. Drop by spoonfuls onto a greased cookie sheet.
6. Bake at 400°F for about 9 minutes, or until lightly browned.

Tips:

- If you like smaller cookies, make the spoonfuls in Step 5 about the size of a level teaspoon.
- I usually bake a cookie sheet full and then cover the rest of the dough and keep it in the refrigerator for a day or so. That way I can have freshly baked cookies.
- Use macadamia nuts in Step 4 for a real treat.

—Barb Yoder, Angola, IN

Peanut Butter Cookies

Juanita Lyndaker, Croghan, NY
Stacy Stoltzfus, Grantham, PA
Joleen Albrecht, Gladstone, MI
Doris Bachman, Putnam, IL

Makes 1–1½ dozen cookies

Prep. Time: 15 minutes ❧ *Baking Time: 8–10 minutes per sheet*

1 cup peanut butter
1 cup sugar
1 egg
Additional sugar

1. Mix the first three ingredients together in a medium-sized mixing bowl.
2. Break dough off with a teaspoon and shape into balls.
3. Roll each ball in granulated sugar.
4. Place on greased baking sheet. Press down with a fork, making a crisscross pattern.
5. Bake at 350°F for 8–10 minutes, or until golden brown.

Deliciously Chocolate Brownies

Alice Whitman, Lancaster, PA
Michelle Martin, Ephrata, PA

Makes 10 servings

Prep. Time: 10–15 minutes ❧ *Baking Time: 28–30 minutes*

2 sticks (1 cup) butter, melted
½ cup + 2 Tbsp. unsweetened cocoa powder
2 cups sugar
4 eggs, beaten
1½ cups flour
Pinch salt
½ cup chopped nuts
1 cup miniature chocolate chips

1. In a mixing bowl, combine butter and cocoa powder until well blended.

2. Add sugar, eggs, flour, and salt. Stir with a fork. (Stirring with a fork keeps the brownies from becoming too cakey.)

3. Stir in chopped nuts. Spread in a greased 9 × 13-inch baking pan.

4. Bake at 350°F for 25 minutes. Do not overbake.

5. Sprinkle with chocolate chips. Return to oven for 3–4 minutes, or just until chocolate melts.

6. Cool completely before cutting with a plastic knife—which will cut clean.

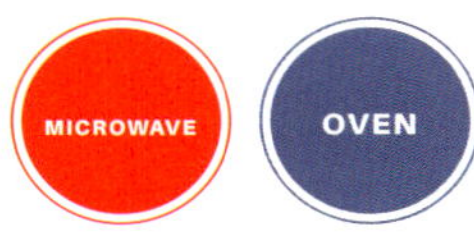

Ultimate Apple Crisp

Judi Manos, West Islip, NY

Makes 6–8 servings

Prep. Time: 15 minutes ❧ *Cooking/Baking Time: 25 minutes*

- 6–8 apples (use baking apples if you can find them)
- 1 cup brown sugar
- 1 cup dry oats, quick or rolled (both work, but rolled have more texture)
- 1 cup flour
- 1 Tbsp. cinnamon
- 1½ sticks (¾ cup) butter, melted
- ½ stick (¼ cup) butter, cut in pieces

1. Core, peel if you want, and slice apples. Place in microwave and oven-safe baking dish (a Pyrex-type pie plate works well).

2. In a separate bowl, mix the brown sugar, oats, flour, and cinnamon. Add melted butter and mix with a fork until thoroughly mixed.

3. Place mixture on top of the apples. Microwave on high, uncovered, for 10 minutes. Let stand for 2 minutes.

4. Cut up the half stick of butter, and place on top of heated apple mixture.

5. Place in oven and bake at 350°F for 15 minutes.

Peach Cobbler

Phyllis Good, Lancaster, PA

Makes 8 servings

Prep. Time: 20 minutes ✤ *Cooking Time: 3–4 hours* ✤ *Ideal slow-cooker size: 5-qt.*

- 3–4 cups sliced peaches
- ⅓ cup sugar
- ¼ cup brown sugar
- Dash nutmeg
- Dash cinnamon
- 8 Tbsp. (1 stick) butter
- ½ cup sugar
- ¾ cup flour
- 2 tsp. baking powder
- ¾ cup milk

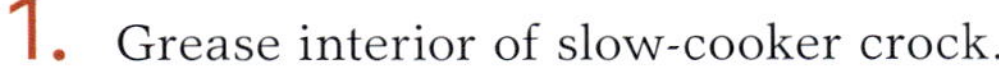

1. Grease interior of slow-cooker crock.
2. Mix together in a good-sized bowl the peaches, ⅓ cup sugar, brown sugar, nutmeg, and cinnamon. Set aside to macerate.
3. Melt butter, or place in slow-cooker crock turned on High and let it melt there.
4. Meanwhile, stir together remaining ingredients in a bowl—½ cup sugar, flour, baking powder, and milk—until smooth.
5. When butter is melted, make sure it covers the bottom of the crock. Spoon batter evenly over butter in crock, but don't stir.
6. Spoon sugared peaches over batter.
7. Cover. Bake on High 3–4 hours, or until firm in middle and bubbly around the edges.
8. Uncover carefully so condensation from inside of lid doesn't drip on the cobbler. Remove crock from cooker.

Serving suggestion:

Serve warm with milk or ice cream.

Cherry Berry Cobbler

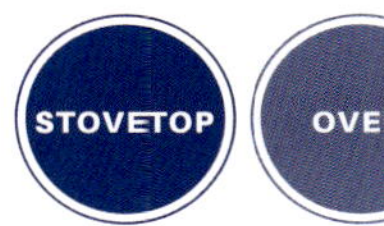

Carol DiNuzzo, Latham, NY

Makes 6 servings

Prep. Time: 10 minutes ♣ *Baking Time: 30 minutes*

- 21-oz. can cherry pie filling
- 10-oz. pkg. frozen red raspberries, thawed and drained
- 1 tsp. lemon juice
- ½ cup flour
- ¼ cup sugar
- ⅛ tsp. salt
- 4 Tbsp. (½ stick) butter

1. Preheat the oven to 325°F.
2. In a saucepan, combine pie filling, raspberries, and lemon juice. Bring to a boil over medium heat.
3. Turn into a greased 1-qt. casserole.
4. In a bowl, mix the flour, sugar, and salt. Cut in butter until crumbly. Sprinkle over fruit.
5. Place the cobbler in the oven and bake for 45–50 minutes.
6. Serve warm (not hot) alone, or over ice cream.

Gluten-Free Four Berry Cobbler

Hope Comerford, Clinton Township, MI

Makes 6 servings

Prep. Time: 10 minutes · *Cooking Time: 4–5 hours* · *Ideal slow-cooker size: 3-qt.*

½ cup sliced strawberries
½ cup blueberries
½ cup blackberries
½ cup raspberries
1 cup gluten-free Bisquick
½ cup turbinado sugar
1 cup milk
½ cup coconut oil, melted

1. Spray crock with nonstick spray.
2. Place berries in the crock.
3. In a bowl, mix the Bisquick, turbinado sugar, and milk. Pour this over the top of the berries.
4. Pour the melted coconut oil over the top of the Bisquick mixture.
5. Cover and cook on Low for 4–5 hours.

Serving suggestion:
Serve over vanilla ice cream.

Greatest Apple Pie

Lynette Nisly, Lancaster, PA

Makes 8 servings

Prep. Time: 30 minutes · *Baking Time: 45–55 minutes*

Filling:

- 1 cup sugar
- 2 Tbsp. flour
- 1 tsp. cinnamon
- Dash nutmeg
- Dash salt
- 6 cups peeled and sliced apples (Rome is my favorite)
- Unbaked 9-inch pie shell

Crumb topping:

- ¼ cup brown sugar
- ¼ cup sugar
- ¾ cup flour
- Scant ⅓ cup solid shortening

1. To prepare filling, combine sugar, flour, cinnamon, nutmeg, and salt in a large bowl.
2. Add sliced apples and mix well. Put apple mixture in unbaked piecrust.
3. To prepare topping, combine sugars and flour in a medium-sized bowl.
4. Cut in shortening with a pastry blender or fork until crumbly. Sprinkle over apples.
5. Bake at 400°F for 45–55 minutes.

Fresh Peach Pie

Lavon Martins, Postville, IA
Darlene E. Miller, South Hutchinson, KS

Makes 6–8 servings

Prep. Time: 15 minutes · *Cooking Time: 10 minutes* · *Chilling Time: 30 minutes*

- ¾ cup sugar
- ½ tsp. salt
- 1 cup water
- 3 Tbsp. cornstarch
- 2 Tbsp. white corn syrup
- 3-oz. pkg. peach gelatin
- 4–6 peaches
- 9-inch baked piecrust

1. In a saucepan, combine sugar, salt, water, cornstarch, and syrup. Cook until clear, stirring constantly.
2. Add gelatin and stir until dissolved. Cool in fridge for 30 minutes.
3. Slice peaches. Place in piecrust.
4. Pour filling over peaches. Chill until ready to serve.

Serving suggestion:

Serve with whipped cream or ice cream.

Key Lime Pie

Norma I. Gehman, Ephrata, PA

Makes 1 (10-inch) pie

Prep. Time: 20 minutes ❧ *Baking Time: 25–28 minutes* ❧ *Chilling Time: 8 hours, or overnight*

- 1½ cups graham cracker crumbs
- ½ cup firmly packed light brown sugar
- 1 stick (½ cup) butter, melted
- 2 (14-oz.) cans sweetened condensed milk
- 1 cup key lime juice
- 2 egg whites
- ¼ tsp. cream of tartar
- 2 Tbsp. sugar

1. Combine first 3 ingredients. Press into a 10-inch pie pan.
2. Bake at 350°F for 10 minutes, or until lightly browned. Cool.
3. In a mixing bowl, stir milk and lime juice together until blended. Pour into crust.
4. In a clean mixing bowl, beat egg whites with cream of tartar at high speed until foamy.
5. Gradually beat sugar into the egg whites until the sugar dissolves and soft peaks are formed, about 2–4 minutes.
6. Spread egg-white meringue over filling. Bake at 325°F for 25–28 minutes.
7. Chill 8 hours, or overnight.

Lemon Pie for Beginners

Jean Butzer, Batavia, NY

Makes 8 servings

Prep. Time: 10 minutes ❀ *Cooking Time: 10–12 minutes* ❀ *Cooling Time: 15 minutes*

- 1 cup sugar
- 4 Tbsp. cornstarch
- ¼ tsp. salt
- ½ cup water, *divided*
- 3 egg yolks, slightly beaten
- 2 Tbsp. butter
- ⅓ cup lemon juice
- 9-inch baked pastry shell
- Meringue or whipped cream, *optional*

1. Combine sugar, cornstarch, salt, and ¼ cup water in 1½-qt. microwave-safe bowl.
2. Microwave remaining ¼ cup water on High until boiling. Stir into sugar mixture.
3. Microwave 4–6 minutes until very thick, stirring every 2 minutes.
4. Mix a little hot mixture into egg yolks. Blend yolks into sugar mixture.
5. Microwave 1 minute more.
6. Stir in butter and lemon juice.
7. Cool for 15 minutes and pour into pie shell.
8. If desired, top with meringue (instructions below) or serve with whipped cream.

Tips:

- To make a meringue, beat 3 egg whites, adding 1/4 tsp. cream of tartar and 3 Tbsp. sugar slowly. Continue beating until stiff peaks form. Cover the lemon filling with meringue to edge of crust. Bake in 350°F oven for 10–12 minutes or until meringue is golden.
- Using the microwave is so much easier than cooking the filling on the top of the stove. You don't have to worry about it sticking or burning to the bottom of the pan.

Southern Pecan Pie

Mary Ann Bowman, East Earl, PA

Makes 6 servings

Prep. Time: 10 minutes ❧ *Baking Time: 50–60 minutes*

Unbaked 8-inch piecrust
1 cup chopped pecans
3 eggs
⅓ cup brown sugar
1 cup light corn syrup
2 Tbsp. butter, softened
⅛ tsp. salt
1 tsp. vanilla extract

1. Place pecans in piecrust.
2. Beat eggs in a mixing bowl.
3. Add remaining ingredients and mix well.
4. Gently spoon filling over pecans.
5. Bake at 350°F for 50–60 minutes, cr until browned and set in the middle.

Variation:

Instead of brown sugar and corn syrup, use ¾ cup honey.

—Charlotte Hill, Rapid City, SD

Shoo-Fly Pie

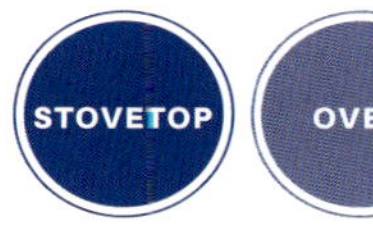

Sharon Anders, Alburtis, PA
Arlene M. Kopp, Lineboro, MD

Makes 8 servings

Prep. Time: 15–20 minutes ♣ *Baking Time: 40 minutes*

Crumbs:

1 cup flour

⅔ cup brown sugar

1 Tbsp. butter, softened

Filling:

1 cup molasses

1 egg

1 tsp. baking soda

1 cup boiling water

Unbaked 9-inch pie shell

1. In a mixing bowl, stir together flour, brown sugar, and butter. Reserve ½ cup of crumbs, and set aside.

2. Add molasses and egg to crumb mixture remaining in the mixing bowl. Mix well.

3. Dissolve baking soda in boiling water. Then add to the mixing bowl, mixing until blended.

4. Pour filling into pie shell and top with remaining crumbs.

5. Bake for 10 minutes at 375°F; then for 30 minutes at 350°F.

Fudge Sundae Pie

Deb Martin, Gap, PA

Makes 6 servings

Prep. Time: 30 minutes ⁂ *Freezing Time: 2 hours*

¼ cup + 3 Tbsp. light corn syrup, *divided*
2 Tbsp. brown sugar
3 Tbsp. butter or margarine
2½ cups crispy rice cereal
¼ cup peanut butter
¼ cup ice cream fudge sauce
1 qt. vanilla ice cream

Tip:
Add chopped peanuts to the top, or whipped topping and maraschino cherries. Use butterscotch topping as drizzle.

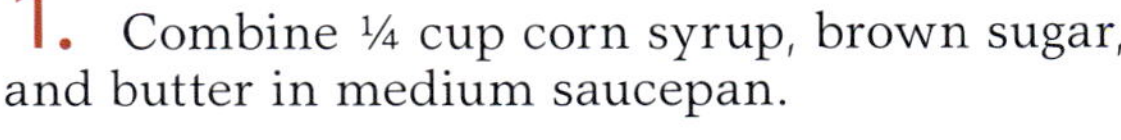

1. Combine ¼ cup corn syrup, brown sugar, and butter in medium saucepan.
2. Cook over low heat, stirring occasionally until mixture begins to boil. Remove from heat.
3. Add rice cereal, stirring until well coated.
4. Press evenly into a 9-inch pie plate to form crust.
5. Stir together peanut butter, fudge sauce, and 3 Tbsp. corn syrup.
6. Spread half the peanut butter mixture over crust. Freeze until firm, 1 hour.
7. Allow ice cream to soften slightly.
8. Spoon into frozen piecrust; spread evenly. Freeze until firm, 1 hour.
9. Let pie stand at room temperature for 10 minutes before cutting and serving.
10. Warm the other half of the peanut butter mixture and drizzle over the top.

Whoopie Pie Cake

Sheila Plock, Boalsburg, PA

Makes 20–24 servings

Prep. Time: 20 minutes ⁂ *Cooking/Baking Time: 20–25 minutes* ⁂ *Cooling Time: 1 hour*

1 chocolate cake mix
1 extra egg

Filling:

8 Tbsp. (1 stick) margarine, softened
½ cup shortening
1 cup sugar
Pinch salt
1 tsp. vanilla extract
½ cup milk
4 Tbsp. flour

1. Mix cake mix as directed on package with the addition of one extra egg.
2. Grease one 9 × 13-inch pan. Pour in half the batter.
3. Line another 9 × 13-inch pan with waxed paper on the bottom and up the sides to use as handles after the cake is baked.
4. Pour the other half of the batter in the waxed paper pan.
5. Bake according to package directions, possibly decreasing baking time because the mix is halved per pan. Check for doneness by inserting toothpick near center of cake. If toothpick is clean, cake is done. Cool at least 1 hour.
6. Make the filling by creaming margarine, shortening, sugar, and pinch of salt in a medium mixing bowl.
7. Slowly add vanilla and milk.
8. Add flour, 1 Tbsp. at a time. Beat on high 5 minutes until sugar dissolves.
9. Spread filling on bottom cake layer in greased pan.
10. To make the top layer, lift the other cake out of pan with waxed paper. Remove waxed paper. Place on top of filling.

Pineapple Upside-Down Cake

Vera M. Kuhns, Harrisonburg, VA

Makes 10 servings

Prep. Time: 20 minutes ⁂ *Cooking Time: 4–5 hours* ⁂ *Ideal slow-cooker size: 4-qt.*

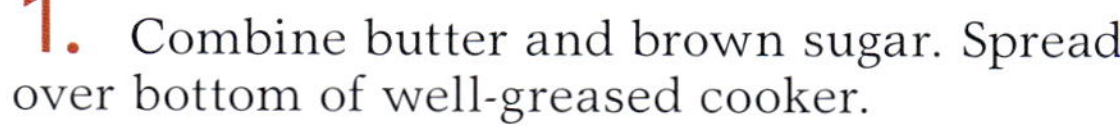

- 8 Tbsp. (1 stick) butter, or margarine, melted
- 1 cup brown sugar
- 1 medium-sized can pineapple slices, drained, reserving juice
- 6–8 maraschino cherries
- 1 box dry yellow cake mix

1. Combine butter and brown sugar. Spread over bottom of well-greased cooker.
2. Add pineapple slices and place cherries in the center of each one.
3. Prepare cake batter according to package directions, using pineapple juice for part of liquid. Spoon cake batter into cooker over top of fruit.
4. Cover cooker with 2 tea towels and then with its own lid. Cook on High 1 hour, and then on Low 3–4 hours.

Angel Food Cake

Pauline Hindal, Grandin, MI

Makes 16 servings

Prep. Time: 10–15 minutes ❧ *Baking Time: 35–40 minutes*

- 2 cups egg whites, at room temperature
- 1⅛ cups flour
- 2 cups sugar, *divided*
- ½ tsp. salt
- 1½ tsp. cream of tartar
- 1 tsp. vanilla extract

1. Place egg whites in the large bowl of an electric mixer.
2. In a separate bowl, sift flour and 1 cup sugar together. Set aside.
3. Add salt to egg whites and beat on high speed until foamy, about half a minute.
4. Add cream of tartar to egg whites. Continue beating until whites are stiff, but not dry, approximately 2½–3 minutes.
5. Quickly sprinkle 1 cup sugar into whites. Beat on a slower speed while sprinkling in the sugar. Then increase mixer to the highest speed, just until the sugar is blended in and very stiff peaks form.
6. Sprinkle in the flour/sugar mixture from step 2 and vanilla. Blend in quickly by hand, using a spatula and a gentle folding motion from the sides toward the center of the bowl.
7. Spoon gently into an ungreased tube pan. Cut carefully through the batter—going the whole way around the pan—with a knife to release large bubbles.
8. Bake at 350°F for 35–40 minutes, or until the top is springy when touched.

Tip:

Do not open the oven while the cake is baking.

Strawberry Shortcake

Joyce Kreiser, Manheim, PA

Makes 15–18 servings

Prep. Time: 8–12 minutes ⁂ *Baking Time: 30–35 minutes*

- 1½ cups sugar
- 4 Tbsp. (½ stick) butter, softened
- 3 eggs
- 4 cups flour
- 4 tsp. baking powder
- 1 tsp. salt
- 1 cup milk
- Sliced strawberries

1. Beat together sugar and butter.
2. Add eggs and mix well.
3. In a separate bowl, sift together flour, baking powder, and salt.
4. Add to creamed sugar mixture alternately with milk.
5. Bake at 350°F in a greased and floured 9 × 13-inch baking pan until lightly browned on top, about 30–35 minutes.
6. Serve topped with sliced strawberries and milk in bowls.

Tip:

Another way to serve this cake is to slice 1½ qt. strawberries into a bowl, sprinkle the berries with 3 Tbsp. sugar, then cover and refrigerate the bowl for ½ hour or more before serving. The sugar over the sliced berries makes a great syrup.

Gluten-Free Pretzel Gelatin

Hope Comerford, Clinton Township, MI

Makes 12 servings

Prep. Time: 1 hour ❧ *Bake Time: 10 minutes* ❧ *Chilling Time: 4 hours or until set*

Crust:

3 cups crushed gluten-free pretzels
1½ sticks (¾ cup) butter, melted
2 Tbsp. sugar

1 cup sugar
8 oz. cream cheese, softened
16 oz. frozen whipped topping, thawed
6 oz. pkg. strawberry gelatin
2 cups hot water
20 oz. frozen strawberries, thawed

1. Preheat the oven to 375°F.
2. Mix the crust ingredients and press them into a 9 × 13-inch baking pan. Bake for 10 minutes and let cool.
3. Mix the sugar and cream cheese. Gently fold in the topping. Spread this mixture over the cooled crust and refrigerate.
4. Mix the gelatin and water until dissolved. Add the strawberries and let cool a bit.
5. Spoon the gelatin mixture over the cream cheese mixture.
6. Refrigerate about 4 hours, or until completely set.

Metric Equivalent Measurements

If you're accustomed to using metric measurements, I don't want you to be inconvenienced by the imperial measurements I use in this book.

Use this handy chart, too, to figure out the size of the slow cooker you'll need for each recipe.

Weight (Dry Ingredients)

1 oz		30 g
4 oz	¼ lb	120 g
8 oz	½ lb	240 g
12 oz	¾ lb	360 g
16 oz	1 lb	480 g
32 oz	2 lb	960 g

Slow-Cooker Sizes

1-quart	0.96 l
2-quart	1.92 l
3-quart	2.88 l
4-quart	3.84 l
5-quart	4.80 l
6-quart	5.76 l
7-quart	6.72 l
8-quart	7.68 l

Volume (Liquid Ingredients)

½ tsp.		2 ml
1 tsp.		5 ml
1 Tbsp.	½ fl oz	15 ml
2 Tbsp.	1 fl oz	30 ml
¼ cup	2 fl oz	60 ml
⅓ cup	3 fl oz	80 ml
½ cup	4 fl oz	120 ml
⅔ cup	5 fl oz	160 ml
¾ cup	6 fl oz	180 ml
1 cup	8 fl oz	240 ml
1 pt	16 fl oz	480 ml
1 qt	32 fl oz	960 ml

Length

¼ in	6 mm
½ in	13 mm
¾ in	19 mm
1 in	25 mm
6 in	15 cm
12 in	30 cm

About the Author

Hope Comerford is a mom, wife, elementary music teacher, blogger, recipe developer, public speaker, Young Living Essential Oils essential oil enthusiast/educator, and published author. In 2013, she was diagnosed with a severe gluten intolerance and since then has spent many hours creating easy, practical, and delicious gluten-free recipes that can be enjoyed by both those who are affected by gluten and those who are not.

Growing up, Hope spent many hours in the kitchen with her Meme (grandmother) and her love for cooking grew from there. While working on her master's degree when her daughter was young, Hope turned to her slow cookers for some salvation and sanity. It was from there she began truly experimenting with recipes and quickly learned she had the ability to get a little more creative in the kitchen and develop her own recipes.

In 2010, Hope started her blog, *A Busy Mom's Slow Cooker Adventures*, to simply share the recipes she was making with her family and friends. She never imagined people all over the world would begin visiting her page and sharing her recipes with others as well. In 2013, Hope self-published her first cookbook, *Slow Cooker Recipes 10 Ingredients or Less and Gluten-Free*, and then later wrote *The Gluten-Free Slow Cooker*.

Hope became the new brand ambassador and author of Fix-It and Forget-It in mid–2016. Since then, she has brought her excitement and creativeness to the Fix-It and Forget-It brand. Through Fix-It and Forget-It, she has written *Welcome Home Super Simple Entertaining, Fix-It and Forget-It Slow Cooker Crowd Pleasers for the American Summer, Fix-It and Forget-It Cooking for Two, Fix-It and Forget-It Instant Pot Cookbook, Welcome Home Diabetic Cookbook, Welcome Home Family Favorites,* and many more.

Hope lives in the city of Clinton Township, Michigan, near Metro Detroit. She has been happily married to her husband and best friend, Justin, since 2008. Together they have two children, Ella and Gavin, who are her motivation, inspiration, and heart. In her spare time, Hope enjoys traveling, singing, cooking, reading books, spending time with friends and family, and relaxing.

Index